A simple guide to
e-commerce

Brian Salter &
Naomi Langford-Wood

Prentice
Hall

An imprint of PEARSON EDUCATION

Pearson Education Limited

Head Office:
Edinburgh Gate
Harlow
Essex CM20 2JE
Tel: +44 (0)1279 623623
Fax: +44 (0)1279 431059

London Office:
128 Long Acre
London WC2E 9AN
Tel: +44 (0)20 7447 2000
Fax: +44 (0)20 7240 5771

First published in Great Britain in 2001
© Brian Salter and Naomi Langford-Wood

ISBN 0-130-28649-4

British Library Cataloguing-in-Publication Data
A catalogue record for this book can be obtained from the British Library.

10 9 8 7 6 5 4 3 2 1

Typeset by Pantek Arts Ltd, Maidstone, Kent.
Printed and bound in Italy.

The Publisher's policy is to use paper manufactured from sustainable forests.

Contents

Introduction . . . . *ix*

What is in this book ix

Conventions and icons x

About the authors x

1 The business benefits of e-commerce 1

Incorporating e-commerce into your business 2

Revenue streams 4

Distribution channels and supply chains 6

Empowering your customers 7

Customer service 8

Global trading 9

Redefining your business model 9

Business-to-consumer e-commerce 10

2 Defining the site 15

Starting to think through your business model 16

Costs 18

Launching an e-business venture 19

Domain names 21

Hosting your site 25

3 Stores and portals 29

What's in it for me? 30

Server-based solutions 32

Software solutions 34

Customer care 36

4 Payments and on-line credit card transactions 39

Credit care payments on-line 40

Merchant services 40

Bureau services 43

PSPs 44

Micropayments 47

Loyalty schemes 49

New currencies 50

5 Internet marketing 53

Search engines and directories 55

Printing your URL 58

Banner advertisements 61

E-mail signatures 64

Word of mouth promotion and newsgroups 64

Site alliances 66

Traditional PR and marketing 67

Portals 68

6 Internet security 71

Transaction security 72

Public key infrastructure 75

Hackers 75

Firewalls 77

E-mail security 78

7 On-line auctions 83

Advantages of selling in an auction 84

Key factors to bear in mind when setting up a Web auction 86

Creating the buzz 87

Setting up your Web auction 88

8 E-procurement 91

Why is e-procurement so attractive? 92

Reducing the workload 93

Getting e-procurement to work 94

An e-procurement example 96

9 Legal points 99

Data protection 100

Taxes and VAT 101

Terms and conditions 102

Disclaimers 102

Contracts with providers of Web services 103

Intellectual property rights 103

Revenue sharing 104
Advertising issues 104
Licensing requirements 105
Trading standards issues 105
Impacts of jurisdiction of the countries into which you intend to sell 107
The e-commerce directive 108

10 Intranets and extranets 109

Intranets 110
Extranets 112

11 The future 115

ADSL 116
Satellite downloads 119
WAP 121
File sharing 122

12 CRM and CMR 125

Demanding customers 126
Flexible companies 130

Mobile customers 131
Products and services that customers really want 133

Index 135

Introduction

The Internet is the fastest growing consumer technology ever created. Throughout the world there are currently some 170 million people on-line with 40,000 new signups *every day*. The proliferation of free service providers has only accelerated the number of new users in the UK and, as the technologies of the Internet merge with those of television and mobile phones, it is not difficult to see the huge potential for doing business over the Web.

The e-business revolution is firmly under way. No business can afford to ignore it. If they do they will be lucky to survive the next few years as the Internet changes the way businesses operate, interact with customers and deal with suppliers.

What is in this book

This book is aimed squarely at business people wishing to jump on to the fast accelerating escalator of e-commerce. It will not contain the answers to all your e-business questions. In such a fast-moving environment that would be well nigh impossible. What it does aim to do is to give a thorough grounding in the principles involved so that you can understand what the experts are trying to tell you without 'snowing' you with techno-speak and other jargon.

Conventions and icons

Throughout the book we have included notes, each of which is associated with an icon:

These notes provide additional information about the subject concerned.

These notes indicate a variety of shortcuts: keyboard shortcuts, 'Wizard' options, techniques reserved for experts, etc.

These notes warn you of the risks associated with a particular action and, where necessary, show you how to avoid any pitfalls.

About the authors

Brian Salter and Naomi Langford-Wood are 21st-century business experts and practical visionaries. Having come from very different backgrounds, they are specialists in all aspects of communication and business usage of Internet technologies and e-commerce and the building of powerful on-line communities; and they are leading international speakers in this arena.

Because of these core skills, they have increasingly found their company in demand for advice on the use of emerging technologies within business, and – in the process – recognised that the cornerstone requirement for all of this commenced with conducting client Internet and communications audits, as a prerequisite to creating effective market positioning and customer focused Internet strategies for these clients. This approach has led to commissions by companies worldwide – both 'blue chip' and SMEs – to undertake Internet audits and consultations for them.

Together, Brian and Naomi help companies realise their full potential by incorporating the new technologies into their business processes as painlessly and profitably as possible whilst looking after each company's core assets – its people. Founders of The Association of E-Business Professionals (**www.e-biz-pro.org**) they are also fellows of the RSA and IoD.

The business benefits of e-commerce

Incorporating e-commerce into your business

Revenue streams

Distribution channels and supply chains

Empowering your customers

Customer service

Global trading

Redefining your e-business model

Business-to-consumer e-commerce

Incorporating e-commerce into your business

With the explosion of on-line businesses and the number of potential customers with Internet access growing exponentially, there has never been a better time to integrate an Internet commerce strategy into your business – unless, of course, we could travel back in time and integrate it *yesterday*.

Traditional bricks-and-mortar businesses are looking over their shoulders and discovering that there's a whole new breed of businesses out there who are rushing to overtake them with the benefit of new technologies to reach out and capture their home markets and steal customers right from under their noses.

The Internet has no geographical barriers, no reason why someone on the other side of the world shouldn't become one of your customers, and equally no reason why you shouldn't be surprised to see your customers disappear elsewhere in search of better deals and better quality products which they can access easily, quickly and cheaply.

Many businesses in the first flush of Internet excitement went out and embraced the new revolution. They set up simple Web sites with quality graphics extolling the virtues of their products – be they physical items or services. And to a degree that has worked well for many companies by giving them a shop window onto a virtual high street that has no physical boundaries and a visibility amongst potential customers who, in the past, would never – could never – have been accessed.

But the world of Internet technology has moved on apace since those heady days of just a few years ago. The development of any business-critical application is always an important factor for any organisation. Where it interacts with your customers, there is no leeway for getting it wrong, and those customers with whom you currently trade may so easily be put off by pages that are slow to download, or that do not give enough information, or whose information is out of date, or that make it difficult for people to make selections and submit orders.

The risk of upsetting your potential clients is not just the lost opportunities, but lost customers, lost business and lost revenue – and potentially the loss of the business itself. Get your strategy right, on the other hand, and you could see your business take off with the benefits of improved productivity, reduced costs of sales, the opening up of new channels and improved profits.

Simply put, e-commerce is the ultimate opportunity in retailing and everybody's opportunity to source the best products at the best prices from around the world. The large, traditional, bricks-and-mortar companies who have for so long dominated their particular markets are now having to rethink their very *raison d'être* and to rework their business strategy in order to fend off the threats from the new kids on the block.

For make no mistake: no business, in whatever sector it may operate, can afford to be complacent about the new risks it will have to face. E-commerce represents the next major revolution, comparable with the Industrial Revolution, or the Guttenburg Press – companies that underestimate its potential will be overtaken by other companies anxious to take on the big boys.

What is needed to compete in this brave new marketplace is the ability to put aside traditional ways of doing business and to think laterally in a way that has not been necessary for most of us in our working lives until now.

In the traditional business model, spending used to be dominated by the costs of wages, transport and distribution, general infrastructure and marketing.

Now that has all changed. People costs still take up a high proportion of outgoings, but the old bricks-and-mortar costs have fallen dramatically in overall percentage terms and the cost of marketing is coming to the fore. There's a whole new world out there with new potential customers, but it is not enough to put a Web site up on the Internet and to hope that they will find you. You need to tell them you exist and encourage them to visit you. And marketing is the key to success in this arena.

In changing your business model to be one jump ahead of the competition, you will need to rethink a number of important areas:

- Your revenue streams
- Your distribution channels
- Your supply chain
- Empowering your customers
- Customer service
- Your global attraction

Revenue streams

It might at first seem strange, but many of today's most successful new businesses have made it big by literally giving away their products. Practitioners of the *open source* model know that there are other revenue streams that can potentially be worth very much more than the central products around which the company appears to be making a market. Consider:

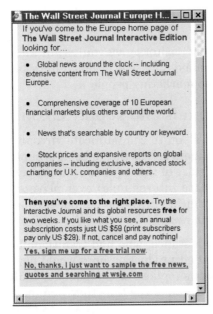

Figure 1.1 The *Wall Street Journal* – example of a subscription model.

- On-line advertising – an obvious example
- Subscriptions to sites that offer useful information (such as some journals – e.g. the *Wall Street Journal*)
- Credit card processing (e.g. Cybercash)

- 'Marriage brokers' where the site acts as a broker between buyer and seller (e.g. property sites)
- Databases – where your visitors give you useful information that can form the basis of a worldwide database of people interested in your type of product – worth millions to marketing people.

Distribution channels and supply chains

Since the Internet allows you to communicate virtually instantaneously with your suppliers and customers across the globe, it is appropriate to rethink your relationships with both sides of this equation. In the early days of e-commerce, when EDI (electronic data interchange) over private networks allowed big companies to deal electronically with their suppliers, one of the buzzwords – or buzz phrases – was *just in time*.

Car manufacturers, for instance, who had traditionally kept weeks' worth of stocks of spare parts so their production lines would never stop, discovered that if they insisted that their suppliers of components could guarantee to deliver these components hours ahead of the time they were needed, rather than weeks ahead, they could save on their cash flow as well as on their warehousing. The Internet offers most of the advantages of private networks without the enormous set-up and running costs. *Just in time* delivery has now become the norm in many industries where e-commerce opportunities have been identified.

Similarly, whereas customers used to be quite content with being told that their orders would be despatched typically within 28 days, the arrival of the Internet has changed all that. Nowadays, a customer expects that if the order is placed today, it will be despatched tomorrow and arrive in two days time.

Empowering your customers

In the 'old world' of the last century, customers were limited by their geography and the time they had available to compare prices from one end of the high street to the other. Today, in practically no time they can compare prices and quality from a wide variety of sources, and comparison shopping is fast becoming the norm.

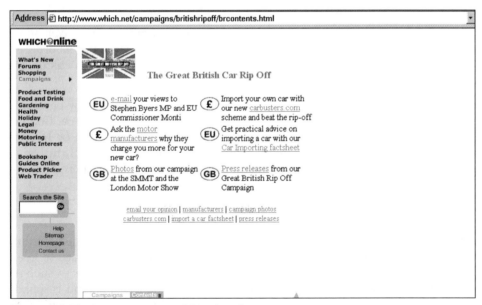

Figure 1.2 The Internet is a powerful medium for campaigns.

One area in which this customer empowerment is most evident is in the selling of cars. For many years, British consumers have complained of the relative high prices of showroom cars compared to the prices enjoyed by their European neighbours. Some entrepreneurs took advantage of the trading rules within the EC to import cars and sell them on in the UK at 'bargain prices'. With the coming of the Internet a number of Web sites have recently opened up selling cars to the UK public at prices up to 30 % below showroom prices.

The car manufacturers, whom many had accused of fleecing their customers, fought back with lower prices if cars were ordered from their own Web sites. Vauxhall, for instance, offered a reduction of £1,000 per car if it was ordered on the Web, but in the first four months of this scheme a mere 125 customers took up this offer.

Pity, then, the poor American car salesman who used to sell new cars at a reduced rate by subsidising the cost with special deals on insurance, finance deals and second-hand car deals. Nowadays all of these things can be bought on the Web and the days of the car salesman – both in the US, but also around the rest of the world – are surely numbered. The dramatic reductions in new and used car prices is testament to the power of the Internet.

Customer service

Since your customer base no longer relies on being geographically hemmed in, it is becoming more important that companies give excellent service to keep their existing customers and to attract new ones. Value-added services such as offering on-line support, answering frequently asked questions, and respond-ing to e-mail requests within minimum turn-around periods are becoming an essential part of e-commerce trading. By automating as many processes as possible in a consumer-friendly fashion, Web technologies can be used to cut costs whilst making life easier for your customers: a win–win situation if ever there was one! But it does need to be well thought through.

Global trading

In the new world of e-commerce opportunities, you need to consider whether you are adequately serving your whole potential client base. In particular:

- Is the use of languages other than English appropriate on your site?
- Are there religious taboos or local customs that could find offence at what is included on your site?
- How will you cope with distribution to these new markets?
- What are the legal implications?

Redefining your e-business model

When using the Internet to simplify and amplify your business, e-commerce normally falls into two main categories: *business-to-business* and *business-to-consumer*.

The former involves the selling of products and services between different companies and the automation of their mutual systems. Using the Internet, time-sensitive information, together with files and applications, can be transferred from one company to another, allowing speedier response times coupled with better accuracy.

If done correctly, business-to-business e-commerce can save substantially on costs and manpower, increase revenue, provide faster response times and delivery, and improve customer service. Indeed, it is not uncommon for the introduction of business-to-business e-commerce solutions in some areas to offer cost savings of up to around 80%.

It is a truism that information is the bedrock on which any business is built, and if you are able to determine your stock levels, goods shipments and total costs more quickly and more accurately, the chances are that you will be able to respond faster in the management of your inventory, buying patterns, distribution channels and staff management, giving you and your shareholders a better return on investment.

Within the next couple of years or so it is likely that e-commerce between businesses will be five times higher than business-to-consumer e-commerce.

Business-to-consumer e-commerce

Most people are familiar with the business-to-consumer e-commerce model. Computer companies such as Dell are selling millions of pounds worth of computers *every day* from their sites. Amazon is probably the best known bookshop in the world, despite the fact that you cannot physically walk through its doors to buy your books and CDs.

It is estimated that fully one third of people buying goods on-line have bought CDs in this way, making this the most searched-for product on the Net. But practically any product or service can now be sourced in this way. That does not mean to say that traditional selling will be eliminated, just that they will have to approach their markets differently.

Figure 1.3 Dell has one of the most successful sites in the world.

Most of the big supermarkets have introduced some kind of Web sales presence – some with more success than others. At the time of writing, Tesco Direct is considered by many to be the most successful, albeit that it does experience occasional teething problems brought on not least by the unexpectedly high take-up rate from its customers.

Sainsbury's, on the other hand, has been floundering badly, not helped by a very strange decision in its early on-line days that insisted that potential customers should first visit a physical store and walk round with a manager selecting the types of products that they might wish to purchase, before being allowed to buy on-line! They finally ditched that scheme, but their on-line store is still difficult to use and has very limited coverage.

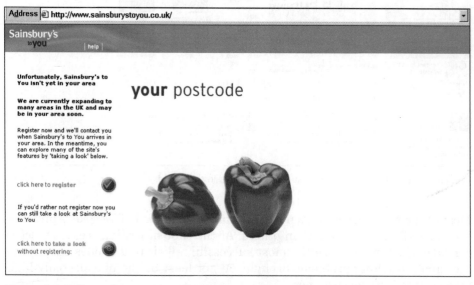

Figure 1.4 Roll out of e-commerce distribution can take a while.

The point is that people are looking for convenience when buying from the Web. The supermarkets typically charge an extra £5 for delivering your weekly shopping, but that hasn't put off the customers. In a society in which time is money, that kind of charge is considered by many to be money well spent.

So business-to-consumer sales provide endless opportunities when using the Internet as long as they are planned right. You can:

- Sell your products and services 24 hours per day, 365 days a year
- Reduce costs associated with retail space and warehousing
- Reduce your wages bill
- Increase your market share and reach new markets
- Compete head-to-head with the big boys with no-one knowing how big a player you are.

With the Internet you can improve your brand or even create an entirely new image, and some of the big brand names are not even five years old.

So what are you waiting for? In the next chapter we will be considering how to set up on the Web and set some realistic goals before being able to trade electronically.

Defining the site

2

Starting to think through your business model

Costs

Launching an e-business venture

Domain names

Hosting your site

Starting to think through your business model

Before going any further, a word of warning: e-commerce is not about fitting a technological solution into your current business. It is not a techie solution looking for a problem. It is a way of increasing your present business – and just so happens to use the benefits of technology to reach that goal.

It is essential to determine both where you are trying to get to and the routes to it. Ignore the latest gizmos that the Internet can offer you. There will be plenty of time later on to consider the goodies on offer, but only once you have worked out what you are trying to achieve.

Start with a vision statement. This sets the tone for what you want to do with your company. Many people have great difficulty in deciding on a vision statement, but essentially it determines your USP (unique selling point) for your business to succeed.

For instance, you might decide to compete purely on price (not, we have to say, a particularly sound long term strategy) or to source products that are difficult to obtain; you might make customer service your focus, or offer a wider range of products than your competition.

Once you have got past this initial stage it is time to set strategies and goals. Remember, it is not necessary at this stage to understand all of the technologies involved. Indeed, it is highly unlikely that your organisation will have the expertise in-house to be able to implement an e-commerce solution. However, when the time is right we will see just where you can find the expertise that you will need. So have patience for the time being.

That having been said, it is nevertheless important that technical expertise is brought into the equation once the goals have been decided upon. Blindly making a decision and expecting the 'experts' to come up with a solution is not always either realistic or beneficial to the organisation.

For example, not so long ago we were called out to a company in Saudi Arabia who wanted to install an intranet on their corporate network so that their 13 office buildings in Jeddah could be linked together. Apart from the obvious benefits of having a corporate intranet (we'll be looking at intranets and extranets in Chapter 10) they wanted to enable live video-conferencing between the different buildings so as to avoid the massive traffic jams that can be part and parcel of life in any major city today.

What they had failed to appreciate is that video-conferencing takes up large amounts of bandwidth. Not only could the local telephone network not cope with the demands of broadband between the different buildings, but attempting to feed video messaging across one of their local area networks practically brought the network to its knees.

One of the most useful things you can do if you are planning to set up an e-commerce Web site is to study what the competition are doing. How else, anyway, will you know if your Web presence isn't just a 'me-too' site, offering exactly what your competition are offering?

You also need to think about who will visit your site and whether they will be able to interact with it in some way. It may be appropriate, for instance, to allow your visitors to order on-line, but equally you might only feel it necessary to offer catalogue facilities to your customers. Either way, do you have a centralised database of stock/inventory or product lines? If so, would it be appropriate to link the site directly to this database so that the site is always up to date? It is now a relatively simple matter to link your site to a database and you could even determine who can access it – making it useful, for instance, for your sales staff to access your in-house data, or even give access to your third party suppliers without letting the 'outside world' into your open house.

Costs

Setting up any kind of business process is going to cost you something, and the Web is no different. There is a plethora of 'free' solutions on offer, but unless you are technically literate and have oodles of time to develop your own e-commerce solution, it is normally better to rely on the experts to put your ideas into practice.

After all, would you design and print your own company stationery, or would you go to a designer and printer and purchase this all for a one-off cost? The Web is not different in this respect. If you want an all-singing, all-dancing Web site incorporating the latest technical wizardry and where design is a premium necessity, then expect to pay anything from £10,000 to £50,000; on the other hand, it is possible to set up shop on the Web, with some 5,000 product lines, all for around £5,000. (We'll show you how in Chapter 3.)

Naturally, the cost of your marketing will be on top of this (see Chapter 5) and this could easily exceed what you paid for the actual site itself.

Launching an e-business venture

We've already stressed that you need first to come up with some ideas, and you also need to research the competition. Only by understanding your position in the marketplace can you hope to come up with some way to make your service unique – the same kind of assessment you would do with any new venture.

The next thing is to get the right people on board at the right time. Often enough, that means getting some people from day one. And network as much as possible. Why reinvent the wheel when you could instead go into partnerships with those who can help you out? No-one can be expected to know and do everything, and 'partnershipping' is often a very cost-effective way of getting all the expertise you need.

Once you have prepared your business plan and have identified the people you need, the next – often tricky – situation is to raise the necessary money to launch your project. Believe it or not, there is a lot of money available to invest in new businesses – whether from a bank, enterprise grants, a business angel network, the Prince's Youth Business Trust or venture capitalists.

It is normal for investors to expect a percentage of your company in return for injecting funds. This can often be a source of resentment, but remember that the investor is taking quite a large gamble in investing in your business in the first place. The majority of start-ups fail, so the risk of losing money on their part is great. It is also better to share your venture in order to make it a success than to keep all the shares and find that the competition outshines you through their being better funded.

*There are now specialist businesses which have been set up to bring together Internet entrepreneurs and investors. One of the best known of these is First Tuesday (**http://www. firsttuesday.com**) which pulls in thousands to its meetings on the first Tuesday of each month.*

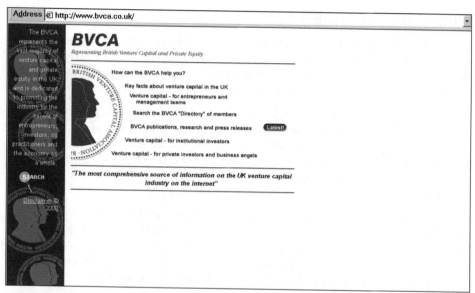

Figure 2.1 The BVCA has helpful advice if you are searching for funding.

Sometimes, the investor will make his money not from a share of the profits the company generates, but from an increase in the value of his investment when the company is floated on one of the stock exchanges, such as the Alternative Investment Market (AIM) or Nasdaq.

If you're looking for an injection of working capital, you could do a lot worse than take a look at the following sites:

- **www.bvca.co.uk**
- **www.ft.com**
- **www.business-incubator.com**
- **www.enterprisezone.org.uk**
- **www.entas.com**
- **www.brainspark.com**
- **www.princes-trust.org.uk**
- **www.ukbi.co.uk**
- **www.atlasventure.com**

Domain names

Assuming you are ready to start, one of the first things you need to do is to register a domain name for your site. It's no exaggeration to say that domain names can make or break a business. Get it right, and it becomes instantly recognisable, but equally there are those who have tried to hijack names or to pass themselves off by using similar names to successful businesses. The courts, both in the UK and in the US, have set precedents that now make it harder for the unscrupulous to make a fast buck at others' expense, but you should always aim to protect your domain name as you would any other aspect of your brand.

Domain name registrations have been opened up since the early days allowing people to register domains in other territories such as Colombia (with **.co**), Tuvalu (**.tv**) or Micronesia (**.fm**). However, the favourite registrations in the UK are still

*One well known case of passing off occurred when the anti-impotence drug Viagra made its appearance in 1998. A porn site called Wetlands registered **www.viagrafalls.com** as a Web name which they used as one of around 120 such registrations to steer users to the main porn site. A Federal District Court in Maryland found in favour of the manufacturers of the drug even though the name Viagra did not appear anywhere on the Wetlands site, nor was the word listed in the site's meta tags to show up on Internet search engines. The decision was based on the fact that trademark owners have a right not to have their registered marks diluted.*

.co.uk, **.com**, **.org**, **.net**, whilst newer domain endings such as **.ltd.uk** are making an appearance as many of the 'best' domain names have been snapped up.

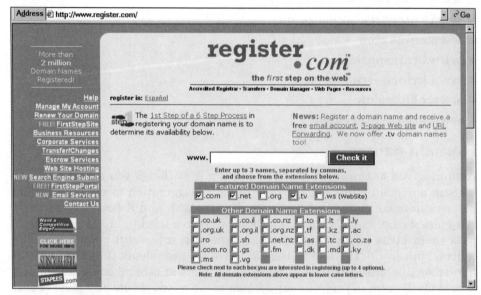

Figure 2.2 Register does just what it says, and you can search too!

*If you want to check out whether your preferred domain name is still available, take a trip to **www.register.com** where you can check out four domain endings at once.*

The costs of registering a name have recently fallen dramatically with some sites charging less than £10 for the registration, as long as you intend to host your site with the company in question. There are hundreds of name registration agents and all the Internet magazines on sale in most newsagents are full of advertisements for domain hosting and registration.

If your preferred domain name has already been taken, try variations such as inserting hyphens or making abbreviations. If you couldn't get www.

Figure 2.3 Did someone forget to re-register…..?

If your site is not being hosted by the company from whom you're buying your domain name, you should ensure that an email forwarding service is included in the price of the name.

brianschocolates.co.uk you could try http://www.brians-chocolates.co.uk/ or www.brianschocs.co.uk, and so on.

Some really cool domain names can be had for the normal price of a domain registration if you find one that has recently expired – that is, someone didn't pay their registration renewal fee on time. For an annual fee of $49, you can get a

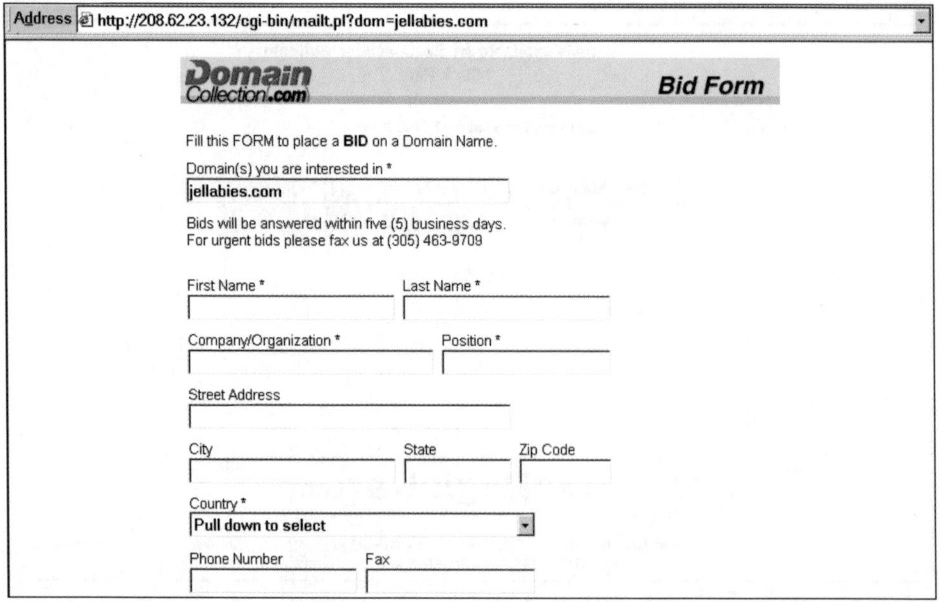

Figure 2.4 ....bids start at $1,950!

weekly list of expired domain names from **www.unclaimeddomains.com**. A well-known international merchant bank was one such casualty and because it 'forgot' to pay its domain renewal fee had access to its all-important Web site cut for two whole days. Meanwhile someone else could have caused a lot of trouble by buying up the domain name.

Hosting your site

Whereas it is perfectly feasible to set up a small site with HTML pages and simple e-mail facilities, the problems associated with success – high traffic, commerce-enabled Web sites – can cause problems with bandwidth, guaranteed up-time and ultimately the company's image.

In such cases it is often a better option to host your site with a professional hosting service. Note that a hosting company is not necessarily the same as an ISP (Internet Service Provider) whose main function is to offer dial-up facilities. Hosting companies are set up to offer server and rack spacing for companies that want to locate their Internet servers outside their offices.

Although the Web host may store your site on the same computer as other sites, the drawback of this is that access speeds may be reduced. If your site is likely to be busy and to dynamically generate output, you will want it hosted on equipment that is not shared with other sites. (You wouldn't want to share a server with the likes of **www.bbc.co.uk**, for instance, since your own site could operate very slowly. If your site is likely to generate huge amounts of traffic it makes sense to consider having a dedicated server.)

The main reason for using a hosting service is to keep things as simple as possible at your end of the business. Running a hosting service is not a job for the faint-hearted and if your business is dependent on the server being useable for as near to 100% of the time as possible, then it really makes no sense to host your own server unless you have round-the-clock maintenance staff available within your company who have the technical competence to deal with all the problems that could arise 24 hours a day, 7 days a week.

So what can a Web host actually offer you?

- First you will get Web space – typically around 50 Mb for a basic minimum configuration, and normally you would expect that to be on a shared computer.
- Most hosts will throw in the first year domain name registration costs.
- You should expect anything from 5 to 100 e-mail addresses included within your overall package.
- Your host should be able to offer e-commerce facilities such as financial transactions.
- CGI scripts and FrontPage extensions will allow your site to handle simple programs to generate dynamic output.
- If your site has database connectivity, ensure that your potential host is able to handle your database software!

Web hosts typically use one of two different types of server software – UNIX or Windows NT. Although you don't need to know the pros and cons of each of these types of software, you should know that, although UNIX is cheaper and easier to run, NT does support extra features such as Active Server Pages and database integration. So if you are planning to offer dynamic content on your site it is well worth letting your host know in advance what it is you are planning to do.

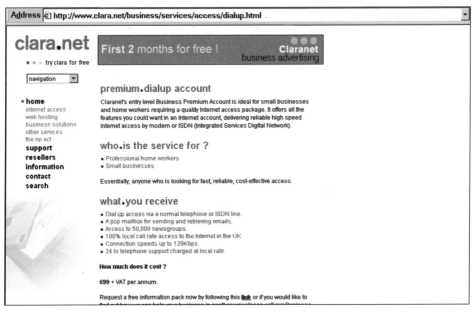

Figure 2.5 Clara is one of many Web hosts offering business dial-up services.

It's also vital that you should be able to get feedback on the traffic generated by your site. Ask your host if it can analyse traffic data for you to provide you with information about who is visiting your site, what pages they are viewing and the route they took to reach your site.

*If you are at all suspicious of the claims made by your host, you can check out its performance by subscribing to Site Reporter (****www. sitereporter.co.uk****) for around £50 a year. You will then be notified by e-mail if your site goes down, or if its access times fall below a certain level.*

Having decided on your hosting service, you now need to consider the intricacies of getting a viable e-commerce site designed and up and running. Meet us in the next chapter to find out how.

Stores and portals

3

What's in it for me?

Server-based solutions

Software solutions

Customer care

What's in it for me?

By anyone's standards, a good e-commerce site is one that makes plenty of sales and/or reduces the cost of sales for proprietor and customer alike. That is stating the obvious of course, but any sales site should aim to sell and fulfil customer expectations from the moment the first visitor arrives.

Fundamental to your entire Web strategy should be the question that will be asked by your potential customers: *What's in it for me?* and *Why should I look at this site at all?*

So why should anyone buy from your Web site as opposed to the thousands of others competing in cyberspace for your prospects' attention?

- Are your prices competitive?
- Is your service exceptional?
- Can you offer a range of products or services that customers actually want?
- Is your site easy to navigate?
- Is the buying process made easy for your visitors?

We'll assume, for the moment, that you will be able to attract your prospects to your site in the first place (and we'll be looking at this knotty problem in Chapter 5).

Start by putting yourself in their shoes. If *you* were a buyer arriving at your site, what would you want?

Don't force your visitors to click more than an absolute maximum of three times to find the product they want. Remember, the more frequently you ask someone to click to another page, the more chance there is that he or she will click away from your site.

Reassure your visitors and address their concerns. For many, the prospect of giving credit card details over the Web to a total stranger is anathema – even though it has regularly been shown that it is much safer than handing your credit card to a waiter in a restaurant. So give them an alternative. Provide your postal address, phone and fax numbers since this in itself can be reassuring.

There are many different ways of setting up a store on the Web. Some are more cost-effective than others and you should consider what you want from your store before going down any one particular route.

For those who are technically minded, you might choose to minimise costs with a do-it-yourself approach. This can work well if you have lots of time at your disposal. However, you have to ask yourself if your time could not be better spent growing the business. You wouldn't necessarily expect to design your business stationery or service your company vehicles, so why should you set up your company Web site?

At the other extreme, there are plenty of solution providers who would be only too happy to design and build a bespoke store to your specifications; but this could prove to be an extremely expensive option.

Don't worry if neither of these suggestions appeal. Fortunately there are plenty of halfway house solutions that are neither expensive, nor will take up far too much of your time.

Server-based solutions

There are plenty of low-cost solutions based on computers known as 'servers' somewhere out in cyberspace. (It actually makes little difference to you where these servers are based.)

Using simple wizards that appear in your browser you can have a simple e-commerce site up and running in a few hours. This is great if you only have a small number of products, but to send the product information to the server can be slow and cumbersome and some people would balk at storing all their product information on a third party's computer at a remote location.

The server-based services all offer templates and differ in their functionality depending on the price you're prepared to pay. Most offer virtual shopping baskets and secure checkout services. Proponents of server-based solutions argue that as your customers are going to access your store through a browser, it makes sense to design the interface in the same way.

Some of the most famous names in server-based solutions are:

- IBM's HomePage Creator (**www.ibm.com/hpc/uk**): IBM prices range from £15–120 per month but it offers a 30 day free trial period.
- BT's StoreCentre (**www.icat.com/affiliates**/): as you can see from the URL, BT's offering is based on *iCat* software which is widely used in the US. Expect to pay around £38 per month for 50 items, or £190 for 1,000 items.
- Web Tool Pro (**www.webtoolpro.com**) starts at £50 per month for 200 items or £130 for 1,000 items.
- Big Step (**www.bigstep.com**) is free of charge – but remember the old adage that you get what you pay for!

■ Shopcreator (**www.shopcreator.co.uk**) costs from as little as £10 with the price rising the more products you have on offer. You can, to a limited degree, alter the look and feel of your site and most of the extras such as a shopping cart facility come as standard.

■ Yahoo! Store (**http://store.yahoo.com**) costs £70 for 50 items and £200 for 1,000 items.

Figure 3.1 Shopcreator is one of a handful of server-based solutions.

With the advent of broadband services and 'free' local call access, it is likely that this type of solution will increase in popularity in the not-too-distant future. Go for this type of e-commerce solution if you want to be up and running really fast without the hassle of installing and learning any software.

So how easy is it to set up a simple store on-line? Yahoo! Store is free for the first 10 days, but the charges start as soon as you want to receive any orders, since until then they will be scrambled!

Starting with a standard grey template (which is actually your home page) you add sections and items for sale following the instructions offered by a Help bar at the top of the screen. You can choose to alter the look and feel of your pages, but only by changing screen colours and fonts. The software puts any pictures you supply where it wants, rather than giving you the option of determining where you want them to be.

The resultant design looks pretty basic, but it does work, and for someone who doesn't have the necessary HTML skills, such a solution provides a very quick way for getting your wares in front of a global audience.

Software solutions

There are also many companies that have developed software solutions which are used by both Web designers and do-it-yourselfers alike and they vary in the number of products they can host, in the number of site designs they offer and the up-front and ongoing costs they charge.

Desktop software is attractive to those who wish to keep their telephone bills low and who wish to use the familiar windows environment. They are easier to

Since all your site building will be on-line and your commands will have to wait until the server responds, it makes sense not to try to build a store in this way during the afternoon period when America has started to wake up. The best time to build a server-based store is in the morning when the Web is operating at its fastest.

integrate into back-end databases and accounting packages and can work out substantially cheaper if you have many products in your store.

The software solutions on offer tend to approach the creation of their stores in different ways.

- Actinic (**www.actinic.co.uk**) is one of the most popular packages on the market. It costs £349 and can handle up to 10,000 items stored in a product database. Included in the package is on-line order processing and credit card security.

- ecBuilder Pro (**www.ecbuilder.co.uk**) costs £299 and has an easy to use wizard. However, it is limited to 2,000 items and it only allows you to collect orders by e-mail which some might not like as it is not a very secure method of trading.

- shop@ssistant (**www.ffloyd.co.uk**) costs £199 and can handle up to 2,000 products, but you'll need to upgrade to the full version (£799) if you want it to cope with more than that.

- AlphaCart (**www.faze.com**) only handles up to 250 products on a maximum of 20 pages, but then it only costs £29.95 since it's aimed at the very bottom of the business market. It also collects orders via e-mail.

- Shop in a Box (**www.ardeo.co.uk**) costs £299 and is incredibly easy to get a store up and running very fast. Its downside is a lack of flexibility and limited layout options.

With all of these packages you enter details of your company and its products, together with shipping rates and any appropriate taxes, and the software creates the site on your hard disk. Once done you upload the catalogue to your Web site and thereafter it's purely a matter of updating your store with any product or price changes. The results can look quite impressive for the amount of time and money involved.

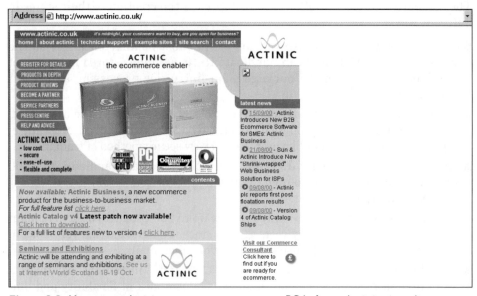

Figure 3.2 You can use Actinic to create a store on your PC before submitting it on-line.

When creating your own store, be sure you are familiar with handling GIF and JPEG images, especially how to optimise them for Web use. Optimisation dramatically reduces the download time needed to load the images into a Web browser. Not least you will almost certainly want to use a scanner to be able to import photographs of your products. Packages such as Paint Shop Pro from JASC software and Macromedia's Fireworks fit the bill admirably in this respect.

Customer care

In a recent report from eMarketeer (**www.emarketeer.com**) the five most important factors motivating on-line buying decisions were listed as:

- Convenience
- Security
- Customer service
- Variety
- Price

The main lesson to be learned from this is that it is important to ensure that your back-end systems are up to scratch and that your customers can always get in touch with somebody in the event that things go wrong.

It really doesn't matter how well you set up your store. Sooner or later things will go wrong, and it is then that you will need to be able to react quickly and efficiently.

That means that if you have stock fulfilment difficulties you should ensure that your customers are kept fully informed since nowadays it is simply not good enough to promise to ship within 28 days. Web culture means that if I order on the Net today I expect it to be shipped tomorrow at the latest and to receive it at the latest the day after.

Surveys of buying habits on the Net regularly report the three main annoyances of customers:

- Merchandise availability
- Shipping and handling costs
- Slow site performance

So, if your service is not up to scratch, remember that there is nothing to stop your potential customers simply surfing away and placing their order elsewhere.

Payments and on-line credit card transactions

4

Credit card payments on-line

Merchant services

Bureau services

PSPs

Micropayments

Loyalty schemes

New currencies

Credit card payments on-line

There are many ways of taking payments on-line and you will have to decide which is the most appropriate for you. For most articles above a certain minimal value, credit cards are the most popular, convenient and easiest to set up.

For those firms that already accept credit card payments for physical transactions it really is very simple to add the extra functionality on-line. You will need to apply to your existing card processor for the necessary authorisations and once they have assured themselves that you already have in place the necessary security mechanisms to avoid fraudulent transactions, the rest should be little more than a formality.

Basically there are two types of transaction processing that they will allow you to use: you can either process the payments manually through your existing systems, or you can opt for an on-line processing system that authorises the payments and transfers the money automatically.

If you are starting out your business on the Net with no physical business to build on then applying for merchant status can take a little time; but the first step is to apply to one of the card acquirers such as Barclays Merchant Services or NatWest Streamline, ask your bank manager, or go to one of the on-line payment processors which operate bureau services. Each have their benefits and downsides.

Merchant services

Whatever the myths surrounding credit card security on the Net, the fact is that banks and credit card acquirers are generally quite positive about Internet

Figure 4.1 Barclays Merchant Services can help you with your credit card handling.

retailing. And so they should be. With the amount of business predicted to be carried out on-line within the next few years, they would be daft not to be.

In general, the risks the banks and card services take are similar to those they would take for servicing any business trading as a mail order or telephone order company. Of course, if you have a trading record behind you, they will be less worried that your business could fail. If you are a retailing virgin they will most definitely want to see a solid business plan identifying the risks – both yours and theirs! They will also want to reassure themselves that you are able to supply your customers promptly and professionally since taking payments for items that you don't actually own, and may have difficulty in sourcing, can be viewed as fraudulent in law.

Risk, to the credit card acquirers, is not just about the fraudulent use of the cards themselves. In practice, the likelihood of hackers intercepting card details on their way from the consumer to your retailing system is very low indeed. And the merchant service providers are generally happy with the use of SSL server encryption (see Chapter 6).

Details of credit cards are much more likely to be stolen from the servers where they are stored, and it is for this reason that most card acquirers will insist that you have suitable firewall protection. This requirement is in line with any other merchant system where you use credit card details to effect a transaction. You will always be obliged to keep cardholder details confidential and to ensure that your systems are protected against unauthorised access.

There are certain categories to which merchant service providers are unlikely to be sympathetic. Pornography – although it accounts for a huge amount of on-line transactions – is one such area, as is gambling. But card acquirers are also unlikely to share your enthusiasm for selling high-value goods, especially those items that can easily be sold on to a third party.

Once you've had your merchant status approved, the next choice you have to make is whether to collect card details from your Web site and then process

According to Visa, credit card fraud on the Internet accounts for less than one tenth of one per cent of all their transactions.

them off-line as you would any order taken over the telephone, or process the payments on-line.

It's far easier to implement an off-line system if you don't have huge numbers of orders, and for many who are starting up an e-commerce Web site it makes sense to handle the transactions manually whilst you get a feel for the amount of transactions you are likely to capture. On-line systems are generally safer for the card issuers because your customers' card details need never come near your system and once you are over a certain threshold of transactions it makes sense to go for this approach.

Bureau services

If the thought of jumping through all the hoops to achieve on-line merchant status does not appeal, you could always consider using one of the many bureau services that allow you to bypass those requirements.

To get the bureau payment system working, you simply add a few lines of code to your Web site which ensures that when customers commit to a purchase, their credit card details are sent automatically to the on-line processor. Full details on how to do this will be given to you by the bureau, who may also offer you the use of a shopping cart facility which you can 'bolt on' to your existing Web site.

Bureau services are usually attractive to smaller businesses who are finding their feet and unlikely to take huge amounts of orders on-line, at least in their formative years. For them, it is usually a safer option than going for the higher risk and higher cost of implementing a bespoke system centred on using a

Although the use of bureau services may seem an attractive route at first, you need to be aware that they typically charge 5% of each transaction in addition to the card issuers' charges; and, depending on the product or service you provide, they can hold on to payments due to you for a number of weeks in order to reduce their risk to fulfilment problems over which they have no control.

secure server, bank-approved software, lease lines to the bank's own systems and specially-written software on top of that.

PSPs

Let's take a look at a live trading facility where money is transferred between your clients and yourself via the offices of a third party bureau known as a Payment Services Provider, or PSP.

Once a transaction has been agreed and the customer's payment details have been accepted by the PSP, the money is transferred from the PSP to you – sometimes in a matter of seconds; other times overnight or after a fixed period of time. Under this type of system you will never see your customers' credit details. They are all handled by the PSP.

The PSP then e-mails confirmations of the order both to you and to the customer and it's up to you to deliver the goods.

Payments differ widely between PSP bureaux but the most basic arrangement is for a monthly or annual fee in addition to transaction charges which are either a percentage of the transaction itself, or a flat-rate fee.

When signing up with a PSP, there are a number of questions you will need to ask:

- **Can you accept simultaneous transactions?** If you suddenly get loads of sales at one time, there is nothing more worrying for the customer than to see what looks like a stalled Web page, and certainly any wait of longer than 30 seconds should be unacceptable. As a rule of thumb, your customers should have to wait no more than 15 seconds for confirmation that their order has been accepted and their payment has been made.

- **Which cards do you accept?** Just because customers in the UK are used to dealing with Visa, Mastercard, American Express or Switch, there are many other nationals who will feel more at home with JCB or Diners Club, to name but two. The Web is an international network and when you set up shop on-line you should always think globally.

- **How long does it take to set up my account?** Although it may be technically possible to have your account up and running within two days, the chances are that your PSP will want to check you out and do some research on your business plan. So don't be surprised if you find that it takes four weeks for you to be up and running.

- **What level of service is guaranteed?** For an on-line trading facility it is important that your PSP can service your customers' demands 24 hours a day, 7 days a week. If there is down time due to technical reasons, what will your PSP do to rectify this, and at what level will compensation be due?

- **What technical support do you offer?** Some companies offer free technical support to their merchant clients, whilst others charge. Make sure you know what your liabilities are!

- **What currencies do you accept?** Some PSPs charge extra for handling multi-currency transactions, but in a global economy it makes sense to ensure you can as a minimum allow your customers to pay in dollars, euros or pounds.

- **How do you handle VAT?** Some PSPs will be able to handle VAT whilst others will not. The problem is that VAT is chargeable on goods sold to clients in any EC country, but not to those outside the community.

- **What are your minimum charges?** Many PSPs have a minimum threshold at which they expect you to trade. Check out what happens if your trade slips below this level, even if only for a month.

Bureaux worthy of consideration

There are plenty of PSPs that offer a reliable and competent service, but the big names you can check out are:

- WorldPay – **http://www.worldpay.com**
- Netbanx – **http://www.netbanx.com**

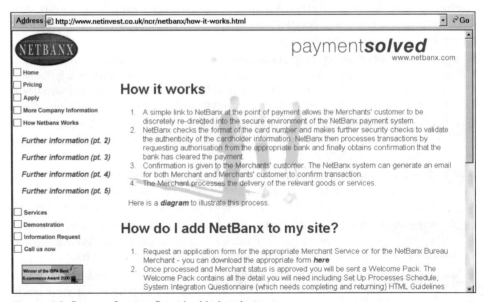

Figure 4.2 Payment Services Provider Netbanx's site.

- Authority – **http://www.radsgroup.com/authority**
- Secure Trading – **http://www.securetrading.com**

Micropayments

Credit cards are an ideal way of paying for goods over the Net, but what happens if the cost of the item for sale is very low? What reaction do you think you would get if you walked into a shop and offered to pay for a packet of Polo mints with your credit card?

Neither shops nor retail Web sites can afford the cost of credit card transactions if the value of the goods is very low. Companies such as CyberCash (**http://www.cybercash.com**) are tackling this issue by processing micropayments in bulk – the idea being that eventually small payments can be bulked together and deducted (or paid) in one lump sum.

Smart cards could also become a force to be reckoned with and used in the same way that some people pay for their gas or electricity – that is, they take their card to a central pay point (such as a post office) and charge them up with, say, £20 worth of credits. PCs could then have a swipe card reader which could determine how many credits you have in your 'account' and deduct the amount owing.

The first significant experiment with e-cash was in 1992 when Mondex launched a trial of its smart card technology using 4,000 employees of NatWest Bank. Staff paid for food in the bank's canteens using their Mondex cards and charged up their cards from ATM machines in much the same way they would have withdrawn cash from a 'hole in the wall'. Three years later the trial was

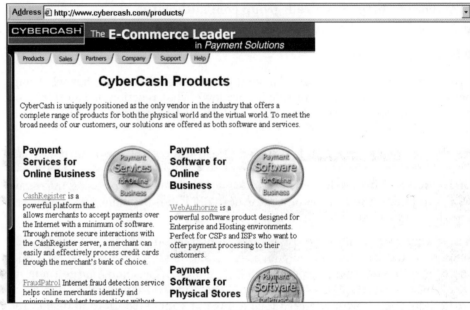

Figure 4.3 If micropayments are a problem … CyberCash comes to the rescue.

extended to cover the whole of Swindon in Wiltshire, equipping some 20,000 people with their own cards that they could use to purchase products in local stores. Currently there are similar experiments taking place in Canada, Hong Kong and the US.

Electronic cash could become the main way you pay for CDs or books on-line, deducting the points from an electronic wallet or purse on your PC. Under such a system, the bank would send you a string of serial numbers representing the cash that it would digitally sign. You would send the digitally encoded 'cash' to the retailer who would forward it to the bank for clearance. There are several companies such as eCash Technologies (**http://www.ecashtechnologies.com**) and eBits (**http://www.oakington.com**) who are now working on such systems. And Visa has introduced 'Visa Cash' offering both prepaid cards (much like phone cards) and reloadable cards (such as the Mondex offering).

Loyalty schemes

Between the hard reality of credit card schemes and the new upcoming micro payment schemes that are still in their infancy, there is a middle ground being introduced by such companies as Flooz (**http://www.flooz.com**), Beenz (**http://www.beenz.com**) and Ipoints (**http://ipoints.co.uk**). With these so-called loyalty schemes, you can earn points for purchasing goods which are then redeemable against other on-line products.

For instance, BT Internet subscribers can collect ClickMiles which can be exchanged for Air Miles or for discounts at other retailers such as lastminute.com. Zoom's loyalty card offers both discounts and access to Webcam fashion shows.

Beenz is a rare hybrid – promoting itself as 'The Web's Currency', you get beenz by visiting sites on the Web (in other words you get 'paid' to visit sites) which you can then spend on goods in other stores.

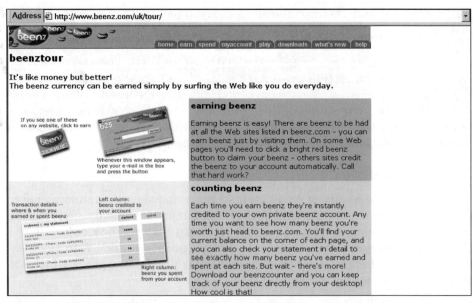

Figure 4.4 Beyond the dreams of average? You too can become a beenz counter.

At the start of 2000, there were around 400,000 Beenz accounts – about one quarter of them in the UK – with some 350 million beenz in circulation.

New currencies

Although many will argue that credit cards are unlikely to be superseded in the next few years, there is a distinct possibility that well known brand-name companies such as Microsoft, Yahoo! and Netscape will set up their own on-line payment systems.

Some would go further still and argue that the future of traditional high street banks is in doubt. Already the German car maker BMW has opened up a bank in Japan where its brand image is exceedingly strong. Phone companies, just like supermarkets, could set up in competition with the banks and use electronic cash to differentiate their product from their rivals. And with all the political commotion over whether Britain would be better off inside or outside the Euro zone, it may in time become a matter of academic argument only as we all gravitate to a universal currency – the global or Web dollar perhaps?

The final killer model for micropayments could be the system already used in Finland where products can be purchased and charged to your phone bill. If you go to Helsinki station and want to purchase a soft drink, you can dial up the Pepsi machine on your mobile phone, tap in your PIN number and receive the can of cola without parting with any money. The crunch time comes when your phone bill arrives, however; not only has the cost of your drink been added to your phone bill, but also a 17% handling charge. This method of instant shopping has found favour not only in station forecourts, but also in golf driving ranges, car washes and copy centres.

Internet marketing

Search engines and directories

Printing your URL

Banner advertisements

E-mail signatures

Word of mouth promotion and newsgroups

Site alliances

Traditional PR and marketing

Portals

According to Forrester Research, spending within the e-commerce market will grow to around $3 trillion by 2003. With so much business up for grabs, it is not surprising that marketing and the build-up of on-line brands is now a number one priority for those trading – or wishing to trade – on the Net.

We all know that oft-quoted *cri de coeur*: 'I know that half of my advertising works; the trouble is I don't know which half'. But marketing is essential to bring people to your site. How else will they know you're there otherwise? (Well, of course, once they are there you need to make their experience of your site and your service an unforgettable and enjoyable experience – and then they will tell their friends and colleagues. But then that's all to do with the marketing experience as well, isn't it?)

Nevertheless it really is staggering how many businesses seem to get their marketing so very wrong – and by that we include the big high street retailers who really should know better. Marketing is fundamental to the way your business runs – and that's true for both e-commerce related businesses and bricks-and-mortar businesses. Failure to appreciate the importance of marketing your e-commerce offerings will precipitate your virtual business into a no-win area.

There are plenty of ways to get traffic to your site. You can (and should):

- List your site on search engines and search directories
- Add your URL to everything you print
- Consider placing banner advertisements on other people's sites
- Take advantage of word-of-mouth campaigns using the Net
- Investigate forming alliances with other sites

- Think about a good PR campaign
- Use the whole range of traditional marketing and advertising routes
- Put your site's URL on your e-mails along with your phone and fax numbers and physical address

Search engines and directories

By far and away the most commonly used method of getting traffic to your site is to list your site in as many search engines as possible. There are well over 600 search engines worldwide, and your aim should be to get listed in at least 10% of them. Some engines are universal in their listings; others deal with specific subject areas only such as travel or commerce; yet others deal only with newsgroups and posted comments (see below).

It is important to understand the difference between search engines and search directories. The former essentially use 'robots' to surf the entire World Wide Web looking for key words and phrases and then making up a huge database for you to access; directories, on the other hand, rely on humans working in real time to input information into their listings so that, to a degree, you get qualified listings of sites under key areas.

This means that if you want to surf, say, music sites in general you might choose to use a directory such as Yahoo! (**www.yahoo.co.uk**) and explore its listings; if you wanted to find out about the Leeds Youth Training Orchestra in particular you would be better off using a search engine such as Google (**www.google.com**); and if you wanted to find a particular recording of Messiaen's Turangalila Symphony you would have most success by using one of the in-site search engines as found on, say, CD Now (**www.cdnow.com**).

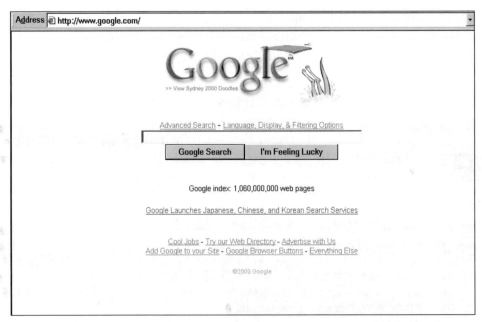

Figure 5.1 One of the best search engines around, Google got into the 'swim' of the Sydney Olympics.

When a company registers its site with one of the directory listings it is asked for a list of keywords which adequately describes what the site is about. It is these keywords that trigger the resultant sites in the search process carried out by the user. Listing a site with most of the directory listings is free – in fact each of the search sites provides a means of registering your details. The search engines will normally just ask for the URL of the site and then point their robots at the site to mine the information for themselves.

Figure 5.2 It's important to tell the search engines that your site exists!

*One of the most convenient ways of registering with several search engines is to send in your details to sites such as Submit-It (**www.submitit.com**) or Add Me (**www.addme. com**) which then automatically inform the majority of the major sites about your details. Some of these sites do, however, charge for this process, but it will ensure your site has the best chance of being found by potential customers.*

If you don't submit information to the search engines, they may well find your site by themselves. You can help them, however, by using what are known as *meta tags* in your source code. These meta tags are not visible to the viewer, but they are quickly spotted by the robot engines. By entering your keywords into these meta tags, the search engines do not bother with simply reading, say, the first 20 words of your home page, but instead absorb the meta-tagged words.

Amongst the most popular search sites are:

- Google (**www.google.com**)
- Alta Vista (**www.altavista.co.uk**)
- Excite (**www.excite.co.uk**)
- Northern Light (**www.northernlight.com**)
- Hot Bot (**www.hotbot.com**)
- Lycos (**www.lycos.co.uk**)
- Yahoo! (**www.yahoo.co.uk**)

Printing your URL

It may seem obvious, but that doesn't stop many people from forgetting that you should add your URL to anything and everything that you print. You wouldn't dream of sending out such material without a phone number, a fax number and an address on it, would you? Well, the URL is just another form of contact address and it, together with an e-mail address, should always be there where it will get noticed. But as a minimum you should include your URL address on:

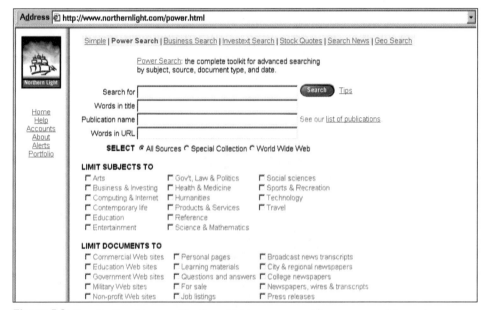

Figure 5.3 Despite its odd name, Northern Light comes up with some powerful searches.

- Headed notepaper
- Business cards
- Packaging materials
- Company vans

- Invoices
- Printed catalogues

The inclusion of those WWW addresses on the bottom of advertising posters and on TV adverts is now regarded as normal. EasyJet even has its URL on the sides of its planes!

Figure 5.4 EasyJet's high-flying advert.

Banner advertisements

The big names in Internet commerce have since the early days (well, 1994 to be precise) invested heavily in on-line banner campaigns. How appropriate is this, though, for the smaller players?

Banner ads differ from printed advertisements in that the latter are normally complete in their own right. In the on-line world, however, the consumer is required to complete a process to get to the information, often thereby leaving the site they chose to go to in the first place. That means that banner ads must be really compelling in the first place to get people to check them out.

Because of the limited amount of information that can be posted in the space of a small rectangle on a computer screen, many banner ads roll information sequentially whilst also having something flying around to attract attention.

Of course, banner adverts can be used for advertising a company's wares, or particular products, or simply to build a brand image. For the latter to be effective, you really do need deep pockets. Normally to build brand awareness you would want your banner ads to be seen in the major portals such as search engines or ISP portals (for example Freeserve or Microsoft Network (MSN)). It requires a long term commitment, exclusivity deals with the portal owners and is probably out of the reach of most smaller businesses at any rate.

But portals and content providers rely on advertising for a large part of their income. They are also experts at targeting their customers. So if you sold, say, financial services, you could pay for a banner ad to be included in the business and information pages of Yahoo. Alternatively you could link your ad to keyword

Banner ads come in various shapes and sizes – typically anything from 88 × 31 pixels to 468 × 60. They will normally have a company name, a slogan or description of a product, and a call to action such as click here. They are usually either a static or animated GIF picture file, although it is now becoming much more common to feature Flash-animated graphics which are great at catching the eye.

searches so that if you were a plumber, you could arrange for your ad to appear every time someone searched a particular search engine for 'tap' or 'washer'.

There are many media companies such as 24-7, Real Media and Double Click which act as brokers for companies and coordinate campaigns across a number of sites, targeting the ads to match the editorial content of the sites concerned. The chances are that if you approach the likes of a large portal with a view to taking out an advertising contract, you will automatically be directed to one of these agencies.

Generally if you want to be able to make use of portal advertising, you should be prepared to spend a few thousand pounds. An ad on Yahoo's home page is likely to cost at least £25,000, but a short campaign to test the market is more likely to cost around £2,000. Either way, you should plan your objectives very carefully and thoroughly check the costs and what you will actually get for your money.

Having said all that, though, it is not actually necessary to pay for banner advertisements at all. If you only have a small promotional budget, you could consider using one of the many banner exchange schemes available. With these, you agree to serve up a banner from other site operators in exchange for having your own banners displayed on other sites. Usually these are automated systems that require members to include pre-prepared code on their sites. You can get information on this type of banner exchange from:

- **www.ukbanners.com**
- **www.linkexchange.com**
- **http://uk.hyperbanner.net/**
- **www.findit-bannerexchange.mersinet.co.uk**

You can get more information on these on-line ad agencies from:

www.247europe.com
www.tsmi.com
www.realmedia.com
www.doubleclick.com
www.nmms.co.uk

Figure 5.5 Banner exchanges are a popular and cheap method of getting your Web site noticed.

Most banner sites offer some kind of statistical roundup of how your banners are being used and how much traffic to your site they are generating. Remember, though, that the more traffic that comes to your site, the more your banner will be displayed on other sites. Also, if banners from other sites contain Java applets or contain heavy graphics, they could slow your site down. But that's a sacrifice you must be willing to make if you want to spread the word in this way.

E-mail signatures

How many e-mails do you and your work colleagues send out every day? When you tot up the number of e-mails emanating from a typical company it surely makes sense to take advantage of the marketing angle that e-mails offer you. The majority of e-mail programs nowadays allow the user to append short text messages at the end of every message sent, automatically. These so-called 'signature files' are at their most effective when short and to the point. They could read something like 'For the latest information on Our Company's products, check us out at www.ourcompany.co.uk'.

If every employee of the company has a similar signature file, your message will in a short period of time be read by an awful lot of people. Better still, change the message on a regular basis – perhaps once a week – so that it continues to get noticed and directs both your potential customers and your business suppliers to your Web site. The more the message is seen, the more it will get remembered, perhaps in the subconscious, and the more likely someone will be to try out your site.

Word of mouth promotion and newsgroups

The 'word on the street' is extremely important for e-commerce sites – more so than for traditional stores. If people get awful service at your site, or alternatively get superb service, the chances are they will tell someone about it. In the on-line world, that might mean mentioning it in a newsgroup where their com-

Although not common at the time of writing, video banners containing mini video films are likely to make a huge impact with the imminent arrival of wide bandwidth and fast downloading served up by ADSL technology (see Chapter 11). However, as a halfway house, streaming video is already being used to display some video banners. Using this technique, the viewer watches the first part of the video whilst the next part is downloading. The trick is to make sure the bit downloading is always there by the time the user is ready to view it.

ments may be seen by typically 5,000 people; or a chat room participant might well tell 100 people. Either way, you shouldn't miss this valuable opportunity – assuming, that is, that your site offers superb service!

Newsgroups can be an ideal source of material for research, especially in relation to customer attitudes. Used with care, they can also be a useful place in which to advise those with an interest in your particular types of products that they can find more information at your Web site.

A strong caveat, however, has to be made because this particular area of the Internet really does shy away from commerce. Indeed, many have learned the hard way that annoying the participants in a newsgroup by posting what are quite obviously commercial messages can result in having their computers 'flamed' by angry or short-tempered participants. On occasions it has been known for so much hate mail to come in that the access provider could not cope with the volume and has had to shut down the service. Even if you don't anger the other participants to such an extent, your commercial message will still be self-defeating since you will be upsetting the very people you are trying to attract.

So how do you market to this ideal captive audience? The answer has to be 'with subtlety'. Obviously you will only target those newsgroups that are clearly relevant to your product or service. Some newsgroups are more opposed to marketing messages than others, and a golden rule if you are thinking about posting a message to such a group has to be to read the messages posted there for a number of weeks before posting your own. It will soon become clear whether your marketing message, however subtle, is going to antagonise the very people you are trying to influence.

If you do decide to go ahead and post your marketing messages onto a newsgroup, be honest about who you are. It is much better – and much less likely to antagonise others – if you identify yourself as working for a company that specialises in the particular topic of the newsgroup and that you therefore have valuable knowledge you can pass on, rather than being blatantly commercial about the wares you are trying to sell.

If your company finds that its products or services are discussed in newsgroups, it is certainly in order to respond. Many of the participants in the discussion are likely to appreciate the fact that your company takes the time to monitor and respond to their comments, but again, keep your comments short, answer the points raised and avoid being overtly commercial in tone. It will have a much greater impact on your audience, and you will also gain valuable marketing feedback in the process.

Site alliances

It's amazing how many companies that rely on other companies to fulfil their orders in some way stop short of actually working with them in publicising their joint offerings. One company we worked with, for instance, made the spray nozzles essential to the atomisers on perfume bottles. Another company supplied the plastic tube through which the liquid travelled and a third company manufactured the bottles. But it never crossed anyone's minds working in these three companies that not only were they *not* in competition with one another, but without the other two, their own product was superfluous.

The obvious thing would have been for a joint marketing effort to have been set up between the three companies so that they could all benefit from one another. In such a situation, it would make sense to have hyperlinks (perhaps banner advertisements) from each of the companies' sites pointing to the complementary offerings from the other two sites, thereby reinforcing the ease with which potential customers could gather pertinent information.

On a much more common scale, there are now plenty of sites – such as Amazon (**www.amazon.co.uk**) – which pay commission to other sites which direct visitors to their own site when a sale results. In consequence, there are now over 60,000 Web sites which direct their own visitors to Amazon and get paid a percentage of any income generated by their visitors. Anyone can apply to become an Amazon associate and both parties gain from such an alliance.

Traditional PR and marketing

Although we have been looking at on-line marketing opportunities, don't forget the more traditional ways of product marketing. In particular, remember the impact made by dot-com companies such as lastminute (**www.lastminute.com**) and Ready2 (**www.ready2shop.com**) by their advertising on the sides of taxis and buses and using posters on the London Underground.

Although lastminute might have been a flop in terms of their share placing, with hundreds of very angry investors claiming they had had a raw deal, at the end of the day lastminute.com is a brand name that is known by practically everyone in this country. Only time will tell whether this will give them longevity.

Figure 5.6 Ready2Shop had a series of stunning adverts on the London Underground.

Portals

If you're on the Internet to sell a product or service, it makes a lot of sense to take advantage of the traffic generated by portal sites to interest visitors in your own area of expertise. The word 'portal' means many things to many people, but essentially a portal gathers together information on one topic or many topics and directs people to other places on the Web where they can get more information on a particular topic.

A good portal should help you find the information you are after on any subject quickly and easily. There are generalised portals that try to be all things to all men; there are some portals that are subject-specific; and in between there are all types of portals too numerous to mention.

By registering your business Web site with different types of portals you have a good chance of visitors finding you when they are looking for information on a particular topic that is linked with your product or service.

The owners of the portals are not in it just to be altruistic. They know that by offering such directory services they can attract traffic to their site; and by attracting traffic they can then charge premium rates for advertising.

So it is no coincidence that the first portals were general search engines. The grand-daddy of them all is Yahoo! (actually a search directory rather than an engine as all its listings are input by people). Although it started off as a simple directory of the best sites covering a wide variety of subject matter, it now offers in addition to that free Web mail, shareable calendars, an on-line address book, a news ticker, personalised messaging and the ability to format information the way you want it by using what they call *My Yahoo!*. You can find this portal at **www.yahoo.co.uk**.

Of the search engine portals, probably the best include:

- AltaVista Connections (**www.altavista.com**)
- Excite (**www.excite.co.uk**)
- Lycos (**www.lycos.co.uk**)

As we mentioned above, there are a number of fine multi-purpose portals that attempt to offer information on very wide-ranging areas. Many of these portals sprang up from the Internet service providers and on-line service providers, and as such some of them guard their content for their own members only. AOL (**www.aol.co.uk**) is one of these that has masses of information, but only if you are one of their members. The majority of Internet users can do a lot better elsewhere.

For the best in generalised portals services visit:

- Freeserve (**www.freeserve.net**)
- LineOne (**www.lineone.net**/)
- MSN (**www.msn.net**/)
- Netscape Online (**www.netscapeonline.co.uk**)

Internet security

Transaction security

Public key infrastructure

Hackers

Firewalls

E-mail security

Fraud on the Internet is widespread. And one of the principal reasons that companies put off having an e-commerce presence is because of fears over security. Of those that have an Internet presence, two thirds of companies in the UK do not use the Net to send confidential or sensitive information.

However, it's important to keep things in perspective. Thanks to encryption technology and well designed firewalls, most e-commerce sites are places where there's little or no risk in handing over your credit card details. How else do you think the likes of Amazon have, for instance, built up a thriving book-selling empire except by being trustworthy places to shop?

Transaction security

Viable standards for secure forms of payment are critical if the success of trade over the Internet is to be assured. Business-to-business transactions often involve high value orders or data which is critical to the running of the firm. And it is for this reason that the majority of these types of transactions are carried out by private network service operators. Frankly, the Internet is just too insecure to guarantee the same levels of data security.

Trading sites, such as retailers, typically accept both credit and charge cards, but the most common mechanism involves prior registration of customers who gives their credit card details as part of the registration process, perhaps by telephone, fax or post. Registered customers are given a password with which to identify themselves when making on-line purchases. However, because of the extra process involved in pre-registering, many sales are lost as the potential client goes elsewhere with his business.

On-line transactions account for around 2% of Visa International's business, but cause half its disputes. In the US some 6m online consumers have been victims of credit card fraud, according to the National Consumer League.

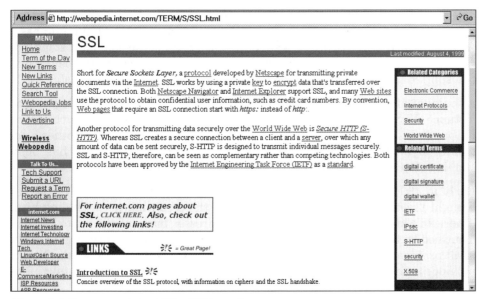

Figure 6.1 You can read about SSL at Webopedia.com.

The sad thing is that passing the details of a credit card number over the World Wide Web is probably safer in the long term than just phoning through the details, let alone having old credit card transaction slips turn up in the waste from a shop or restaurant. However, in this game, perception is all and no business can afford to be seen to be taking risks in such a sensitive area.

It wasn't long ago that the amount of computing power required to crack a 40-bit encrypted message was horrendously large. But with the advent of faster and more powerful computers, decrypting 40-bit keys is now possible by many hackers. In 1998 a machine known as Deep Crack was built which was capable of searching some 92bn encryption keys per second. It could crack a 40-bit key in six seconds. However, a 56-bit code would take it nearly five days, whilst a 128-bit key would take this machine many millions of lifetimes to crack. For this reason, 128-bit encrypted SSL is now becoming the de facto protection for e-businesses.

To try to meet this concern there has been much work to evolve common standards of transactional security between the two parties involved in a purchase. A system called SSL (Secure Sockets Layer) has become the dominant standard. Here the purchaser fills in an electronic form. This is then encrypted before it is transmitted to the vendor, who is the only one who can decipher the details.

A number of on-line trials are taking place using different technologies. For instance, Visa and Bank of America have been using the Visa Cash chip card for payments under $10 (£7) whilst both organisations are testing other electronic payment systems. Mondex, as mentioned in Chapter 4, has been trialling electronic payment systems for some time now.

Early in 1996 a new standard called SET (Secure Electronic Transactions) brought together many of the big players in the credit market including Visa, American Express and Mastercard. SET addresses many of the major worries identified by business users. Specifically it ensures confidentiality and integrity of all payment and ordering information that is transmitted across the Net, it provides authentication of both the user and the vendor and it is totally platform independent.

SET may play an increasing role in Internet-based transactions (although to date its impact on e-commerce has not been dramatic) as long as the transaction is suitable for credit card dealings. However, many are unsuitable because the amount of money involved is so small – perhaps pennies at a time (known in the trade as 'micropayments') and the commission that would be charged by credit card companies would therefore be disproportionately large (see Chapter 4). To meet this problem head-on, a number of electronic currency payments – over 50 at the time of writing – have been developed.

Perhaps the best known is First Virtual (**http://www.fv.com**). Set up specifically to target business use of the Internet, this is a bank that gives its clients a password in exchange for their payment card details. The purchaser uses this password to authorise payment over the Net. First Virtual then charges the user's charge card and passes the funds on to the vendor, minus its own commission.

Public key infrastructure

In order to guard against people posing as others on the Internet, a system of public key cryptography has been developed and more are being worked on all the time. The certificates used in SSL Web servers are based on a few trusted authorities such as Verisign or Thwaite.

An alternative is used by the freeware program PGP (Pretty Good Privacy). This mixes public key cryptography with a traditional passworded system using public keys to encrypt the message key. More details can be found at **www.pgpi.com**.

Hackers

Of course, many of the problems of Internet security have little to do with the transfer of money. Simply being connected to the Net carries inherent risks if your company computer is in any way connected on-line. There are legion stories of companies having valuable data stored on internal computers interfered with in some way by outside hackers, causing the disruption of internal communications, changing or deleting some of the information, or accessing confidential files. One of the most famous attacks in recent times was

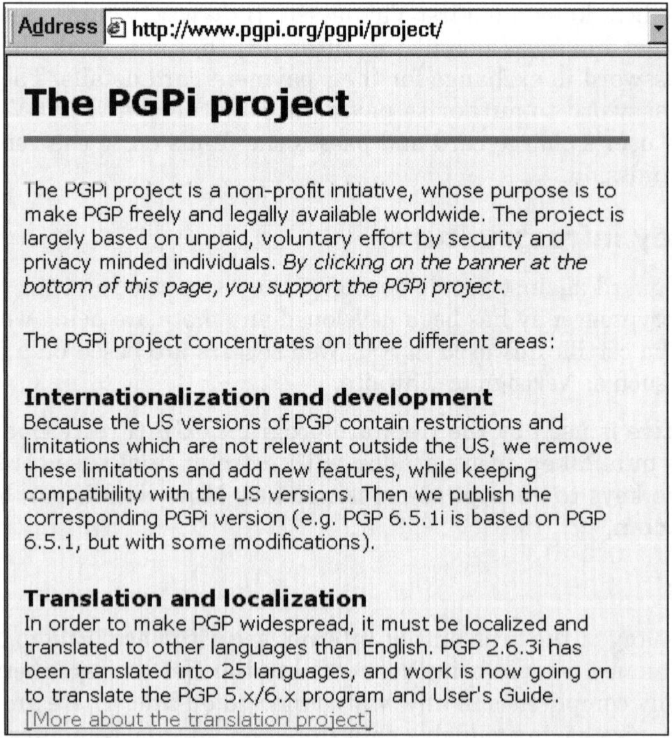

Address http://www.pgpi.org/pgpi/project/

The PGPi project

The PGPi project is a non-profit initiative, whose purpose is to make PGP freely and legally available worldwide. The project is largely based on unpaid, voluntary effort by security and privacy minded individuals. *By clicking on the banner at the bottom of this page, you support the PGPi project.*

The PGPi project concentrates on three different areas:

Internationalization and development
Because the US versions of PGP contain restrictions and limitations which are not relevant outside the US, we remove these limitations and add new features, while keeping compatibility with the US versions. Then we publish the corresponding PGPi version (e.g. PGP 6.5.1i is based on PGP 6.5.1, but with some modifications).

Translation and localization
In order to make PGP widespread, it must be localized and translated to other languages than English. PGP 2.6.3i has been translated into 25 languages, and work is now going on to translate the PGP 5.x/6.x program and User's Guide.
[More about the translation project]

Figure 6.2 Pretty Good Privacy has the edge when it comes to encryption.

perpetrated on the Web site of the Labour Party when pictures of prominent figures were replaced by pornographic images and some of the accompanying text was replaced with defamatory allegations.

The threats of hacking generally fall into three main camps:

- Denial of service – where servers are flooded with requests that slow down its connections with others on the Net
- Intrusion – where servers are penetrated by hackers who then manipulate data
- Viruses – program code that will usually damage or delete data on the server

Usually the hackers only do this in order to brag about it to their friends, rather than do criminal damage; but it can be expensive and frustrating to have to put things right and repair your system. Hackers also can break in to a company network and plant viruses which may be simply a message that pops up to announce that an infiltration has taken place, or at the other extreme a little program that destroys much of the data held on the system. Small- and medium-sized businesses are particularly vulnerable to hacking because they often do not bother to invest in the necessary protection.

Firewalls

The mechanism that has been developed to control such access is called a 'firewall', named after the bulkhead used to protect aircraft and ships from engine fires. This is a computer or router that stands between the company's internal network and the Internet. Only data which is authorised by the firewall is allowed through. Any person or data without proper identification gets turned away.

There are basically three types of server firewall: starting at the lower end of the scale 'packet filters' cost around £2,000, a mid-range system known as 'circuit level' will set you back around £5,000 and top of the range systems known as 'application gateways' come in at tens of thousands of pounds. A firewall works by examining the format of packages of data which pass through the communication channel. Each package carries a source address and that of the destination machine and it is this that allows the firewall software to check these addresses against a database of permitted users.

In addition to tracking the access of data into and out of the company, firewalls can also track who is connecting to the company server and this allows the system administrator to set up special guards against suspicious activity, such as someone trying to get in using a number of different passwords.

E-mail security

As it stands, using e-mail for company business is anything but secure. Your messages pass across many different networks on the journeys to their destinations. At any one of these nodes your e-mail can be intercepted and read. Admittedly, the likelihood of this happening is small once it has left your company, but not impossible.

Whilst it is still within your company's internal system, however, there are many who can quite easily access your e-mail contents. Think about it. Perhaps now is the time to issue content guidelines to your staff, indicating what may or may not be communicated via e-mail, in the same way that you should already have a policy on other forms of communications. Remember that there are risks to the image of a company and its legal integrity if employees do not consider the possible consequences of what they send. A company could find itself legally responsible, for instance, for any libellous statements included in an employee's e-mail sent out from the company's server.

Indeed, there is a false sense of security about internal e-mail which has already been tried in law in the July 1997 case of Western Provident Association versus Norwich Union where the court found for WPA and awarded damages and costs of £450,000 because of libellous e-mails sent internally at Norwich Union. WPA's Chief Executive, Julian Stainton, was quoted as saying: 'People regard electronic mail as a transient medium in that the message disappears into the ether. The reality is that everything you type and send is recorded almost for all time and is available to be reassembled at a later date by the written or spoken word.'

In another case – this time in the US – between Andersen Consulting and UOP (Allied Signal and Union Carbide), UOP sued Andersen for $100m, alleging breach of contract and fraud, based on an exchange of e-mails between the two parties.

On a lighter side we know of one company in which the amorous e-mailed 'pillow talk' between two employees (who presumably assumed that their missives were private) was made very public indeed by one of the IT staff and caused red faces all round!

The problem is sometimes made worse by the fact that many believe – wrongly – that they can remain anonymous on the World Wide Web. Simply removing or changing the log-on details on your e-mail software does not allow you to hide your identity and many have been caught sending what they thought would be anonymous messages, but which were very easy to trace back to their originators.

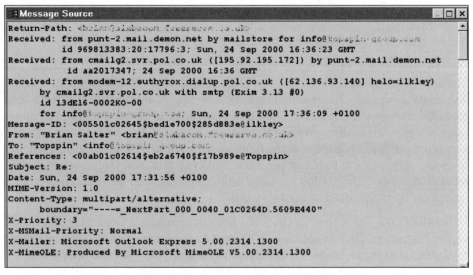

Figure 6.3 All e-mails leave a complete audit path in their peregrinations, which cannot be fudged.

Here are some ground rules for corporate e-mail which will help it run without glitches:

- When communicating with partners and customers treat e-mail in the same fashion as other forms of correspondence – e.g. include the company registration number and registered name and address. This helps to authenticate the document.

- Make the recipient aware that confidential information is being sent. This warning enables you to protect your confidentiality.

- Impress upon your staff that, because e-mail produces a record which is absent in telephone conversations, statements made in an e-mail can give rise to unexpected obligations placed on the company.

- Businesses should make it clear to all staff that misuse of e-mail – either sending abusive mail, distributing unauthorised materials such as viruses, or flame-mail – will be subject to disciplinary action.

- The monitoring of e-mail sent to or from staff is only allowed in law where the sender is aware that interception may take place. If you intend to monitor e-mail traffic you should therefore make it perfectly clear to staff that this could happen; this follows the pattern set by legislation over monitoring telephone conversations.

Again, it is all really common sense business usage that needs to be applied to the new electronic media.

On-line auctions

Advantages of selling in an auction

Key factors to bear in mind when setting up a Web auction

Creating the buzz

Setting up your Web auction

7

When thinking of a traditional business model on the Web we usually think of on-line retail stores selling our wares to customers from all parts of the globe. But there is growing popularity in an alternative way of selling – that is, on-line auctions.

Think of it from a customer perspective. On the Web, the customer is king. He can compare prices from retail outlets around the world, he can order from anywhere, and with delivery mechanisms improving all the time, he can usually expect his ordered items to arrive within days, rather than weeks as was the norm with mail order shopping until quite recently.

Advantages of selling in an auction

From the business perspective, there are also many advantages to selling using dynamic pricing.

If a product is in short supply then an auction can often bump up the price to a realistic level depending on how many people want to buy it. If you don't know how much you should charge for a product or service, an auction is a useful way of 'testing the water' and seeing what people will be prepared to pay for it. Auctions also ensure that bidders pay what they are willing to pay for the item, whilst sellers get the best possible price.

Depending on whom you believe, predictions for the amount of transactions carried out within the booming e-commerce sector are as high as $1 trillion for the year 2002. What is less arguable is the fact that those companies that can integrate dynamic pricing into their new business models are most likely to succeed in their overall strategies.

Dynamic pricing occurs when buyer and seller determine the price for goods on a transaction by transaction basis. Apart from auctions, obvious examples of dynamic pricing are trading on a stock market, or buying goods in a souk.

In addition to high repeat-purchase rates, auction sites tend to be 'sticky' in that customers tend to stick around for longer and come back more often and this can be used for generating advertising revenue because, for the advertiser, there will be more impressions and longer viewing times.

Another positive factor for on-line auction sites is that businesses want to learn about the buying habits of their customers. Web auctions provide the perfect way of doing this as potential interests, bidding methodologies, price sensitivity and other purchasing information can be gleaned quickly and easily.

As well as the advantages to be gained from dynamically pricing your goods or services, on-line auctions have other benefits:

- You can create a new on-line community. (eBay and QXL are two companies that now receive some of the highest trafficked sites every day.)
- Bricks-and-mortar auction houses are moving on-line to extend the reach of their customer base. Sotheby's, for instance, now gets proportionally higher bids for its sales than it did before joining the Web revolution.
- They can maximise inventory revenue. Using a Web auction you can more easily manage overstocked items, establish a market for refurbished and damaged goods and establish true market prices for one-of-a-kind items.
- Business-to-business exchanges are being set up which automate the process of setting prices such as in the spot markets for gas and electricity.
- Requests for proposals whereby suppliers need to bid for contracts can be time-consuming both for the proposer and the contractor. Auctions can cut down the time and paperwork needed on both sides of the bid process.

Figure 7.1 Ebay – first of breed.

Key factors to bear in mind when setting up a Web auction

As with any Web-based business, companies have to be customer-focused and have a well-designed Web site as well as offering secure trading facilities and ensuring that they can deliver goods in a timely manner in sound condition.

Market focus is essential, and focusing on a vertical market is one way to boost a Web auction's success rate. For instance, selling specific goods or services or concentrating on a particular customer type are more likely to gather momentum than sites which try to be 'all things to all men'.

A *sound marketing plan* is also essential in order to gather customers to your site in the first place. In this respect, an auction site is no different from any other Web-enabled retail outlet.

As first impressions count, a *well-designed Web site* gives a feeling of comfort to visitors tempting them to come back again and again. Factors to consider here include easy navigation, plenty of information and the inclusion of appealing graphics.

Obviously you will need *adequate levels of stock* otherwise there will be little to tempt visitors to return. Ebay, for instance, has more than two million items for sale in more than 1,500 categories.

Creating the buzz

If you have ever visited a traditional auction – be it for rare antiques, cars, houses, or whatever – you cannot fail to have been aware of a feeling of excitement generated in the auction room. Selling via and on-line auction is no different if you get it right and there are some basic rules for upping the buzz around your auction site.

- You should actively promote rare or exceptionally popular items.
- You could actively promote the bidding activity on a site by quoting current bids, the amount of bidding activity and final bid prices.

- You can e-mail interested parties whenever a price break has been reached, a reserve price has been met or if someone's bid has been surpassed.
- If you start the bidding low you can attract passing interest. You might make a slight loss in the early stages, but this can be counteracted by the extra publicity this could generate.
- If you set the duration of bidding to be quite short you can create the perception that there is limited supply of your goods, leading to greater interest amongst potential purchasers.

Setting up your Web auction

Until quite recently the only way of setting up an on-line auction was to custom-build one, which could cost many thousands of pounds. Today there are a number of software products available which present packaged solutions, and there are even companies that can set up and administer your auction site for you. It isn't necessarily cheap.

On the other hand, Bidland.com doesn't charge a set up or monthly hosting fee, but instead takes 5% of all sales generated from the auctions. Ariba.com charges its customers based on the number of transactions and servers they need. Some larger sites buy the services from auction vendors and then 'sub-let' them out to others or host their own sites in this way.

However you build your auction site, you will still come across the age old problem that just because you have a site doesn't necessarily mean anyone will come and visit it. Many of the auction technology companies are solving this dilemma by aggregating all their own individual customers' listings on one main site – in effect, making a huge auction portal.

To see some real-world examples of auction sites, point your browser at:

www.ebay.co.uk
www.opensite.com
www.qxl.com
www.bidland.com
www.ariba.com
www.moai.com

Address m/cgi-bin/QXLPage?Auction&type=List&session=339882927&language=EN&category=1066&pageno=1&lines=20

⊘ All Sellers   ① Individuals   ✳ Star Seller   ● Merchant Partner   ⓠ QXL Direct

all auctions are listed in order of closing - next to close is top of list. Times are GMT

status	item	seller	bids	language	ends
📷	**Secret Service Phone Card**		£10.00	⊕	29/09/2000 01:26
	60+ Hungarian Telephone Cards		£100.00	⊕	29/09/2000 19:00
	Circus Posters - Set of 10 Phonecards		£8.00	⊕	29/09/2000 23:27
	TITANIC - Puzzle set of 8 Phonecards		£8.00	⊕	29/09/2000 23:28
	Batman - Puzzle Set of 4 Phonecards		£4.00	⊕	29/09/2000 23:29
	British Steam Trains - Set of 8 Phonecards		£6.00	⊕	29/09/2000 23:30
	Startrek- Puzzle set of 8 Phonecards		£8.00	⊕	29/09/2000 23:32
	X FILES PHONECARDS SET 1		£8.00	⊕	05/10/2000 16:00
📷	BOYZONE PHONECARD		£3.00	⊕	05/10/2000 20:15
📷	BOYZONE PHONECARD		£3.00	⊕	05/10/2000 20:15
📷	ROBBIE WILLIAMS PHONECARD		£3.00	⊕	05/10/2000 21:00
📷	TOP GUN PHONECARD		£3.00	⊕	06/10/2000 18:30

Figure 7.2 QXL has thousands of visitors looking for the most obscure bargains.

Whichever option you plump for, look for flexibility in your site design. You might not know the best type of auction to go for in the initial stages, so it's important to be able to change the rules and the setting up of your site over time. Basically an auction involves a feedback mechanism, and if you cannot act on the feedback you are getting, then you are effectively killing your site stone dead. So talk to your solution provider and get them to assure you that you have control of the site at all times.

Look also at customisation options since you don't want your site looking the same as everyone else's. In common with on-line retail shop all-in-one packages, the boxed software should offer you ways to customise your final Web site. If it doesn't, then look elsewhere for your solution.

Check also for credit card payment systems, ways to rate your sale items, bidder notifications and especially ways in which the software can give you feedback on the things your clients are getting up to – their buying patterns, pages visited, and so on.

It's useful if the software offers promotional additions such as the possibility of displaying banner adverts about particular offerings within the auction; and of course it's essential that the site can scale upwards with higher volumes of traffic.

Whatever path you choose, though, it's important that your vendor – be it a site administration company, an auction hoster or complete solution provider – can support your expanding needs. Most auction sites start out small and grow in time so ensure that migration and upgrades are easy to manage a few months down the line.

E-procurement

8

Why is e-procurement so attractive?

Reducing the workload

Getting e-procurement to work

An e-procurement example

In the last chapter we saw how the use of auction sites can bring buyers and sellers into closer contact with one another so that both sides can enjoy cost savings in their transactions. Larger companies in particular can enjoy massive cost savings in their purchasing if they have an on-line procurement system in place, but this in no way cuts out the smaller concerns.

Typically in the past a company sourced its suppliers from directories such as Yellow Pages, or by collecting business cards at exhibitions, and then putting out tenders for essential supplies to a number of these organisations, matching the returned prices against one another to find the best deal. With an auction site, you specify what you want using an on-line purchasing request form and then your requirements are matched against a supplier database. The supplier decides if he wants to bid for your business; the buyer gets suppliers that can genuinely meet your needs, and doesn't have to waste time on those that can't.

One issue that could make companies nervous about using such sites is the question of security. In theory other suppliers could use the site to discover what their rivals are charging and then use that information to undercut them. Normally, however, the bids are only visible to the buyer although other suppliers could, of course, register as interested buyers and get information that way.

Why is e-procurement so attractive?

Imagine the scenario. A company board meeting has two proposals put before it. One proposal is that the company sets up a Web site in order to display and sell its wares. It is hoped that significant revenues will result from the setting up of this site, but it is felt that it will probably take a couple of years for it to generate enough sales for it to be 'in the black' and start paying for itself.

The other proposal on the table is for an e-procurement strategy whereby all company purchases would be bought on-line and the payback period would be only a few months with a contribution to the bottom line within the first year.

If you were one of the directors, which would you plump for?

Well, we've already seen that an e-commerce enabled site can generate significant revenues for the company over a period of time, but no organisation can afford to turn its back on the opportunities for sourcing via the Web.

The figures of possible savings are impressive for large corporations, but even small companies can make significant cuts in their expenditure budgets by using e-procurement.

Of course, electronic procurement is not a new phenomenon. Large companies such as car manufacturers have been using EDI systems to streamline their supply chain for years. But the real breakthrough has come with the arrival and take-up of the Internet, which has made such systems available to all. Even major corporates such as Ford are transferring their e-procurement to the Internet and away from their proprietary EDI systems.

Reducing the workload

At its simplest, e-procurement offers buyers the chance to automate the routine of purchasing and at the same time eliminate errors. Staff time can be reduced and management can get a far better idea of the amount it is spending on individual items as well as the breakdown across individual departments or different branches. This alone can offer management major opportunities to review where its cost base really lies, and thereby create efficiency savings across the company.

The American giant Oracle claims that its clients such as Boeing, Hewlett-Packard and Pepsico typically enjoyed savings of around 400% on their initial outlay within the first year of using their system, and that, overall, costs of purchasing have been cut by around 5%.

In the UK, Tony Blair set a target for Whitehall departments to save £1 billion from its annual £9 billion procurement budget. With tens of thousands of supplies and millions of transactions a day, the system is ripe for massive savings. The biggest problem in Whitehall – as the Government readily admits – is the poor communication between individual departments; so it could mean that by setting up a universal procurement system for government, one of the side benefits will be a marked degree of closer cooperation between individual departments.

By cutting out off-contract purchasing – whereby employees make purchases at prices other than those negotiated centrally between company and supplier – companies can typically save around 10% on their procurement bill. Providing an e-procurement environment encourages the use of centralised buying and cuts out the problem of go-it-alone mavericks.

Suppliers, likewise, can make cost savings in their tendering process and reach customers at lower cost than has traditionally been possible using 'old fashioned' marketing media. As far as individual employees are concerned, the whole process can be much less bureaucratic and far more efficient.

In short, it's a win–win–win situation.

Getting e-procurement to work

There are three possible models for an e-procurement system to function effectively:

1. A company could host a supplier's catalogue on its own internal intranet, allowing the supplier to update it either via an extranet connection or else by supplying CDs for uploading to the system. Employees would then be allowed to order products directly from the catalogue within laid down guidelines from the company. This is a common model in the US where, not surprisingly, e-procurement is already streets ahead of Europe in this regard.

2. A company could have hyperlinks on its intranet to sites hosted by suppliers. Either the hyperlinks would lead to pages specifically set up for the use of that company only (including any negotiated deals or approved products), or purchases could be ordered from anywhere within the supplier's site, but

Figure 8.1 Letsbuyit.com works on the principle of bundling together prospective buyers to beat down the price on bulk purchase.

would then go to the company's purchasing department for approval and collation. (This way, if an employee decided, for example, that he or she 'needed' a new leather swivel chair, the purchasing department or other control centre could stop the transaction if they thought it inappropriate.)

Errors are cut out because items do not have to be individually entered over and over again and paperwork is reduced to a minimum. Until recently, using traditional paper orders, up to 45% of invoices in the National Health Service were queried. Trials of e-procurement systems within individual NHS trusts have reduced this dramatically.

Although e-procurement appears superficially to be able to obviate the need for human contact in the buying process, the fact is that personal contact helps the establishment of trust between two parties. Using auction bidding for instance, doesn't help establish any kind of trust between the purchasing organisation and the supplier, and for this reason many avoid auction sites for their purchasing. One way round this can be for large companies (at any rate) to pre-approve suppliers bidding on their own auction site, or for smaller ▶

3. The third model uses an auction site for suppliers to compete against one another for your business. This is still a new model in Europe, but is becoming increasingly common in the US.

Some would argue that none of these three models caters for the supply of one-off purchases such as the installation of an office lift, or the installation of air conditioning; however, it is instructive to note that what used to be seen as one-off purchases such as life insurance are already being sold this way in the US. In this model individuals can put their details up on the Net, effectively saying, 'my details are so-and-so and I want quotes for life insurance'. Insurance companies then bid for their business.

An e-procurement example

For over three years the American conglomerate General Electric has been sourcing its raw materials electronically. Not only that, but it also uses the Web for negotiating office leases and contracting staff.

Its annual on-line spend is in excess of £3bn and using e-procurement it estimates the savings it is making to be around 10–15% – or over £300m.

Anyone can apply to be a supplier to GE. Their Web site at **http://www.ge.com** allows would-be suppliers to register free of charge whence they are given a private area for laying out their stall. When GE's buyers are looking for a specific item they post this to each private supplier's area and invite tenders. Suppliers then return an electronic form with their sealed bids and receive feedback on how the bid is progressing.

Not only have the costs of processing orders been reduced by between 50% and 90%, but new suppliers have been found, especially in Eastern bloc and Third World countries, who have proved to be much cheaper in their asking prices.

Staff, meanwhile, use the company's intranet to browse catalogues and send their orders directly to the purchasing department for authorisation and consolidation with orders from other departments and a purchase order is automatically raised.

Of course, the above model only works for large companies, typically turning over in excess of £30m. But, as we mentioned above, smaller companies can effectively club together in their purchasing through brokerages such as Industry To Industry (at **http://www.itoi.com**) where both purchasers and suppliers have to pay a registration fee to cover the cost of vetting them to ensure they are reputable. ITOI takes a commission of between 1% and 8% depending on the size of the order.

However, ITOI ensures the wheels of commerce turn smoothly by having arrangements with Dun & Bradstreet who ensure the companies' status and finances are up to scratch and that would-be partners are not fly-by-night companies; Bureau Veritas and SGS inspect the goods to ensure quality; Danzas organises the logistics and distribution of the goods; and Deloitte Touche Tohmatsu looks after import and export taxes and all the paperwork.

continued

companies to make their procurements through third-party purchasing organisations who are better able to vet each supplier and still pass on savings gained through purchasing in bulk.

Legal points 9

Data protection

Taxes and VAT

Terms and conditions

Disclaimers

Contracts with providers of Web services

Intellectual property rights

Revenue sharing

Advertising issues

Licensing requirements

Trading standards issues

Impacts of jurisdiction of the countries into which you intend to sell

The e-commerce directive

You may well feel that the reams of legal issues surrounding any business become greater by the day and certainly the issues arising from the nature and impact of the Internet and e-commerce demand careful scrutiny in order for a business not to be vulnerable.

In these *new* realms, the levels of possible exposure for businesses are often not seen in advance simply because this is uncharted territory.

In essence we now need to review each area of business and where there is a need for change.

Data protection

The Data Protection Act of March 2000 requires that all companies and organisations who hold a database must register with them. To do this a company must identify what it has the database for and what it intends to do with it. For instance, we heard of a membership organisation which had registered as being one that was intending to write to its members to advertise its services but not allow others to have access to the members' names and addresses. It then did a very foolish thing and gave the whole database to a US-based membership organisation who published a directory of the UK members' names, partial addresses and e-mail addresses. E-mail spam was rife from the recipients of the US-produced UK directory and the governing body had many complaints levelled against it. The release of the database was contrary to their registration with the Act and their members were none too pleased with the outcome. The Internet makes data gathering and, by extension, data dissemination so easy that it is all too common for people to overlook the legal aspects.

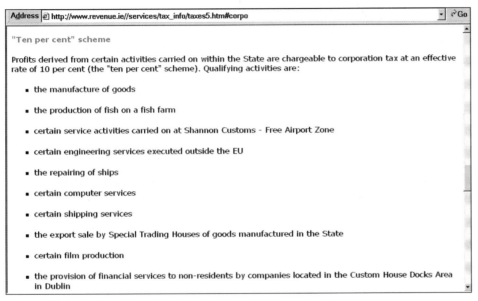

Figure 9.1 Ireland's tax system is the envy of many in Europe.

Taxes and VAT

Taxes apply to the location of the servers on which the Web site or e-commerce site is hosted. Therefore, at the time of writing, the best place for an EU company to have a site hosted is in Luxembourg because their level of VAT is the lowest in the EU (15%). However, as far as corporation tax is concerned you'd be better off having your whole operation based in Ireland as their equivalent of Corporation Tax is currently 10% in some categories. The normal rules and regulations apply with regard to export and tax officials are watching very carefully to ensure that the tax *they* need to stay in business is collected!

Terms and conditions

Whatever your standard terms and conditions are, they need to be reviewed *before* you embark on e-commerce. What are perfectly acceptable terms and conditions in the UK may well not be acceptable in the markets in which you may hope to trade through the Internet. For this, a cool look at the prospective marketplace will ensure that your marketing is stepped up in jurisdictions in which your legal cover is clear. Likewise the payment terms by which you have always run the business may not be acceptable in other jurisdictions. You may well need to renegotiate with your suppliers and customers in this regard.

Disclaimers

Those verbose instruments beloved of lawyers and surveyors may well have no validity at all when posted on the Web for the global market to read. At the moment the interpretation of what is valid and what is not is very much along the lines that if you have put something up on the Web in, for instance, English, then it must be assumed that you are intending any English-speaking person in the world to be a prospective customer and therefore you must think through the multinational implications of the legal issues. No disclaimer will automatically apply to other jurisdictions.

Contracts with providers of Web services

Advertising on the Web site and any implied compliance of service from another party to promises made on your site could get you into trouble. For instance, whilst you may say, in all faith, that a particular courier service will be that used to deliver goods, it could be that you fall out with that named contractor or have not got their permission to state your company's implicit reliance on them. What if they are bought out by another company and decide that your business is just too small for them or in some other way does not fit? Advertised contracts and alliances need to have full approval of all the parties involved prior to being published on the Web if you are to save yourself a potential problem in the future.

Intellectual property rights

Intellectual property is a difficult area to deal with. So many pieces of intellectual property have become almost generic in their common English usage – like Hoover, meaning vacuum cleaner, and Elastoplast, meaning sticking plaster – that you have to think very carefully about the use of some terms. It is very tempting to think of using some of them in connection with your Web site. Some companies have, for instance, got into trouble over using copyright and trademarked terms as 'meta tags' and then found that these useful identifiers are actually a breach of another's trademark.

Because of the intangible nature of intellectual property it is essential to think through step by step any licensing agreements written so that the intellectual property of your firm, as well as that belonging to others, is not compromised.

Revenue sharing

The Internet has brought with it many opportunities to build associations. In fact, the only way for many businesses to keep up with the technology is to form partnerships and revenue-sharing agreements whereby the skills and products of one business are complemented by the skills and products of another. This way time is not lost by having to reinvent the wheel and the perception of comfort of the association gives added value to the original product. However, as lawyers have always said, 'Partnerships are the rockiest ships that ever there are' – and rub their hands with glee because of the likelihood of fallout and dispute. However, most law firms are partnerships so they probably judge other people differently from themselves!

Nevertheless, agreements must be reviewed carefully if you are not to find your company on the rocks because of something that was overlooked or that you thought would not happen because the relationship was too good to be spoiled by either party.

Advertising issues

Oh dear! The number of matters you have to address grows and grows. A Web site, whether for e-commerce or just as an information site, is actually publishing – but publishing on the Web rather than in paper form. A review of any advertising issues is essential to ensure that you have not overlooked important factors like advertising standards. The rules and regulations regarding lotteries and gaming as well as the definition of what are called 'free gifts' and the regulations surrounding competitions are a minefield dismissed by the foolhardy. The laws of libel are onerous and extremely expensive and time-consuming to either prosecute or defend, so a wary look at the whole of your site with the avoidance of libellous statements in mind is essential to avoid problems later.

Licensing requirements

The laws regarding consumer credit, cooling down periods and the licences needed to offer goods and services which fall under the various Acts must be considered. A brief identification of the various products and services you offer will give you an easy judgement as to whether your existing guidelines and processes cover the e-commerce side too.

Other licences, such as those needed for the supply of music over the Internet, have been covered by the cases involving Napster and MP3. Major music publishers have come to an agreement that they will be responsible for collecting the royalties to pay back to the copyright holders and musicians. The same kind of adjustments are having to be made in all areas of business.

Trading standards issues

Any products which you are currently selling will have to be reviewed with regard to trading standards legislation in the different nation states or jurisdictions. With trading standards it is most important that the wording covering the products and services is not ambiguous, thereby leaving your company open to customers' misunderstanding of expectations. When purchasing over the Internet it is not normal to see the goods prior to purchase

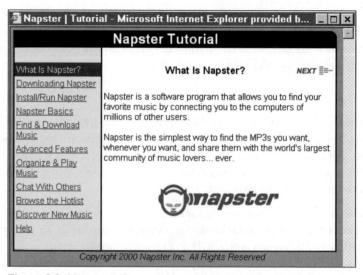

Figure 9.2 Napster stole a march on the music industry moguls.

(as opposed to the usual scenario when buying in a shop where the customer can not only see but often handle the goods). A customer's ability to visualise is often key to his perception and expectation of what is being bought. Accuracy of description and graphic representation of the product must be of paramount importance when selling on the Web.

Impacts of jurisdiction of the countries into which you intend to sell

This is one of the most difficult things to deal with. With e-commerce your company must think globally and act locally. You may well think you have a ripping wheeze and want to offer a guarantee across all the countries to whom

Figure 9.3 Achtung! Land's End hit a German competition law minefield.

your products are aimed, which should give you a marketing edge over the competition. But think again. A classic example of this was Land's End, the clothing merchants, who give a very good guarantee indeed that their clothing is of a particular quality and this guarantee has an extended time on it without further payment from the purchaser. Land's End came a bit of a cropper in the summer of 2000 when selling to Germany because the German competition laws identified that the Land's End guarantee gave the company an unfair advantage and was therefore deemed to be unfair competition for the German companies. Land's End had to withdraw their guarantee as far as German consumers were concerned.

The e-commerce directive

This became law on 8th May 2000, and has issues which will come to light as the EU sorts them all out. The fact that they are law already but that not many people know about them makes the legal issues surrounding e-commerce likely to be something that a business trips up on.

Basically, though, if taken from the premise 'think global – act local' the Internet gives business the ability to reach customers the world over. If you put up a site in French, for instance, then you are presumed to be trying to sell into French-speaking countries. For that you should adhere to the local laws of French-speaking countries. If your site sports English then the same applies as far as English-speaking countries is concerned. If Spanish then you not only have to think of EU laws and the local laws in Spain but over half of South America too – and so on.

With such a lot to do, a well-thought out and timely implementation plan is essential, as is a review as you go along. For all that, it won't be long before every business is an Internet business and the Internet is just another business tool.

Intranets and extranets

10

Intranets

Extranets

Intranets

The effects of using Internet technologies within a business are sometimes more dramatic than those outside. Whereas the World Wide Web was set up to enable any computer to talk to and share information with another one connected via the Internet, an *intranet* is similar except that it operates at a local level allowing users on a local area network to share data using Internet technologies.

The important point is that any computer of any platform can access the network with these technologies. So, PC users can share data directly with SUN users, UNIX platforms, Apple Macs, Acorn RISC stations and a wide variety of other proprietorial systems. The whole point of having an intranet is that it enables people right across an organisation to talk to one another and access commonly used information thereby making the business more dynamic with resulting efficiencies.

An intranet can make huge differences by tapping the resource of shared knowledge that many organisations literally ignore or disregard giving those organisations a cutting edge against the competition. Yet many intranets are developed by IT departments who may be technically literate, but who have no knowledge of the way in which company employees may want to share the information. As such, many are doomed to failure before they even begin.

In an e-commerce scenario, the use of intranets can radically enhance the way in which you can interface with your clients by pooling knowledge gleaned by one member of your staff with that of every other. In a call centre model, for example, the use of intranets is now obligatory and savvy customers know that what they have told one operator should be on record for all other call centre assistants to access. Yet it is truly staggering how many wasted customer interface opportunities exist even within those companies geared up to handling customers on a large scale.

Call centres apart, however, a well-defined intranet can pay dividends when offering easy retrieval, use and management of information and they are particularly well suited to project management applications. By using your intranet you can manage workflow to ensure that each step of the project is completed in the shortest possible time whilst reducing errors.

Figure 10.1 You can even get an intranet for free by going to the Intranetics site.

But go right back to basics when thinking about setting up an intranet for the first time. Ask your people what they would want to use it for. They will be the ones using it, and if all it will do is to keep an internal phone book and copies of HR manuals it is bound to fail.

A well-designed intranet, on the other hand, can do wonders for any business. In one company we went into to carry out an Internet audit, we were able to identify immediate savings of around £30,000 p.a. after only a few minutes. This particular firm operated from three locations and was forever having to make copies of designs for use by different departments which were then couriered across on disk or, by the enlightened few, via e-mail. With the provision of an intranet where designs could be parked by the originating department and pulled off by the users, huge savings could be made overnight.

On a different scale, but one that was nevertheless a boon to those involved, the provision of 'Webcam' cameras around the building meant that the receptionists could easily identify if various people were at their desks in a large open-plan office *before* attempting to route telephone calls to the individuals concerned. If they weren't there, an electronic message could be posted to the recipient informing them of the call and thereby ensuring excellent customer appreciation of the company.

These were but two of many recommendations implemented by the firm involved and the benefits could be felt almost immediately.

Extranets

If an intranet can dynamise your business, just think what it could do were you to make its benefits available to your suppliers and customers. Here we're talking about extranets – the utilisation of Internet technology for a closed-user group intranet available outside the organisation.

Basically an extranet is an intranet that allows remote access, usually, but not always, through the use of a firewall. The main factor in moving up to an extranet is how much trust you place in your suppliers, partners and customers.

There are two main ways in which you can set up an extranet. With the one, you have a normal Web site accessible through the World Wide Web with passwords given to your key customers to allow them to search for more information from specific directories. Alternatively you can offer secure access to an intranet through a specific dial-up route giving your visitors individual access privileges on entry.

They are useful when dealing with orders from trusted customers and when setting up supply deals with trusted partners and third party suppliers. Note the use of the word 'trusted'. The efficiency gains alone from this type of operation make extranets a must-have solution for many firms.

Imagine: Your key customers can log in to your site; they can browse amongst your products and then place their orders on-line. The orders go through to despatch and at the same time the billing department is sent the correct details for automatic raising of invoices. By eliminating human intervention you can make the whole process flow more quickly and more efficiently with fewer errors in the process. It has to be every business owner's dream scenario.

An extranet can prove to be a major key for any organisation to gain competitive advantage – except that very shortly it will be the norm for firms involved in e-commerce to implement such a solution, so perhaps we should really sum

You can also make use of extranets for collaborative projects. Many international courier companies, for instance, allow their customers access to their extranet by going to their Web site and inserting their despatch number so that they can find in an instant where in the delivery process their package is.

up by saying that no serious e-commerce contender can afford to ignore the option of an intranet or extranet.

The main concern with setting one up will be guaranteeing security. You certainly don't want anyone to invade your internal computer systems where they could wreak havoc on your business. However, with careful planning, involving every member of your staff in the planning process, and by putting yourself in the shoes of your suppliers and customers and asking what they would want, you can pay for the initial outlay very quickly.

A final word: don't just assume you know what your customers want. Ask them! You may be surprised by what they tell you.

The future

ADSL

Satellite downloads

WAP

File sharing

A week in politics is a long time, but – equally so – the Internet changes on an almost daily basis. Predicting the future is well nigh impossible, but even if our crystal ball can only peer around the corner there are some exciting things about to happen in the world of e-commerce.

ADSL

By the time you have picked up this book, ADSL (Asynchronous (also known as Asymmetric) Digital Subscriber Line technology) should be up and running in many parts of the UK. At the time of writing, however, ADSL has had endless delays in being released, although it has been a fact of communications life in the US for some time now.

What is ADSL? Simply put, it provides a very fast access route to the Internet which will go a long way to dismissing the old hyperbole about WWW standing for 'world wide wait'. Data will be transmitted 20 times faster than anything your standard 56k modem can offer, and you won't have to wait for your modem to dial up the ISP either since ADSL is effectively 'switched on' all the time.

The advantages of using ADSL are many. For your potential customers, download speeds will be increased dramatically allowing you to put up more complex (and more appealing) graphics on your Web site without your audience clicking away because they get tired of the download wait. You will be able to provide streaming audio and video, making your site more attractive and eye-catching and effectively merging the experience of the Web with consumers' experience of television, making the distinction between the two much more blurred. In fact, in the next few years the two media are likely to converge to a point where it will be difficult if not impossible to tell one from the other.

ADSL uses a standard telephone line, complete with its copper 'local loop' to the exchange. It's because of this copper bottleneck and the fact that the speed of connection is dependent (among other things) on the distance the signal has to travel to the ADSL node, that only those who live within about 3 km of the node will be able to use ADSL.

Many have accused British Telecom of dragging its heels with the implementation of ADSL. By autumn 2000 only around 500 of the country's 5,500 exchanges will have been kitted out for ADSL – and that at a speed of only 512 kbps even though ADSL can run very much faster at typically 1 or even 2 Mbps. The industry regulator has given BT until July 2001 before forcing it to allow others into its exchanges to offer their own services. So expect available speeds to improve dramatically within the coming months.

That said, BT has also come under fire for what is referred to as the 'contention ratio'. Imagine driving along the M25 in the middle of the rush hour and compare that to what you would experience at 3 am. As far as speeds are concerned you're talking about an average 5 miles an hour (if you're lucky!) compared with a theoretical maximum of 70 mph. So it is with ADSL. The more users there are accessing the same ADSL 'pipe' the slower the whole data transfer will be. BT is proposing to allow up to 50 users per 'pipe' for domestic customers and 20 for business customers. But critics argue that there should be a maximum contention ration of 6:1 and that ADSL cannot possibly be of value with 50 users all trying to access their files at the same time. So bear this in mind when deciding whether your business would benefit from the switch to ADSL.

ADSL is not the only way to get on-line fast – by a long way. For those who haven't the means to use ADSL, there is also cable – for those who live or work

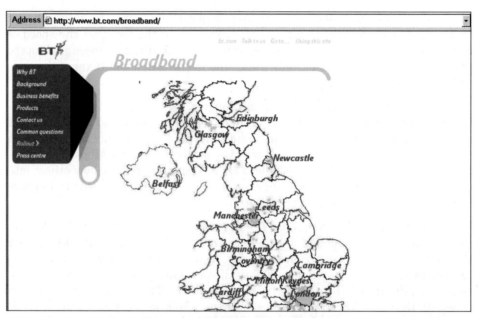

Figure 11.1 Go to BT's site for information about ADSL roll-out; but don't hold your breath.

on a route laid down for cable TV. NTSL is one of the cable TV companies that is already offering high-speed access to the Internet over its optical fibre network.

For larger businesses, especially, there is also the option of installing a permanent 'leased line' from BT, which offers high-speed connectivity – at a price.

This is not likely to prove attractive to smaller businesses unless they require very fast access, or unless they host their own Web server on their premises, in which case a fast, clean line with ample bandwidth is a necessity.

Satellite downloads

Satellite downloads are also becoming more of a reality. For the past few years it has been possible to download large files at fast speed from satellites – such as Eutelsat – but in the next couple of years a host of satellites are to be launched by a company called Teledesic (**www.teledesic.com**) which will effectively offer fast Internet access from anywhere in the world, including remote areas which currently have no effective Internet access at all. The consequence of this is that it should be possible to offer true global Internet roaming from your one ISP account, rather than having to find a local ISP who can link you in to your e-mail and company server. In addition, it is highly likely that it will offer up the potential for new markets as those who have only had limited, expensive or no access at all will join the Internet revolution and have the potential to become your new customers. Think of the effect this will have on your future business prospects!

We mentioned at the start of this chapter that TV and the Internet were converging rapidly to the point where it will soon be difficult to tell one from the other. What that means in practice is that TV is set to become an active medium, rather than catering for a world full of couch potatoes. TV content will not just be supplied by the TV companies; rather viewers will demand to view what they want, when they want, where they want.

Figure 11.2 Teledesic has plans to encircle the globe.

Some TV executives foresee the provision of a local hard drive on TV sets to allow viewers to record content and watch what they want at whatever time it suits them. It won't just be about time shifting programmes, however, since this is effectively what the provision of VCRs has done for a long time. Instead you will be able to watch a football match, for instance, and decide which camera view you want to watch; and along with each programme will be Web pages giving background and further insights into the programme being broadcast.

WAP

At the other end of the spectrum is the provision of Internet services using mobile phones. It's still very early days to predict what will be happening in this sphere but a great deal of effort, not least by the mobile telephone companies, is being expended on WAP and its successors.

At the time of writing there is a great deal of confusion in the minds of the public about just what WAP (wireless application protocol) offers. This is hardly surprising since in the summer of 2000 WAP suffered from slow data transfer rates (typically 9.6 kbps) using GSM (Global Standard for Mobile communications) on phones using very small monochromatic screens. When compared with typical modem transfer rates which are four times as fast on high-resolution screens in full colour it is hardly a surprise that the hype surrounding WAP could not possibly stand the test of reality.

By early 2001 GSM will have given way to GPRS – General Packet Radio Service – offering a permanent 60 kbps connection to a mobile communications device. (At least, that's the theory. In reality, speeds are likely to be much lower, in the order of 26 kbps.) And a couple of years later, UMTS (Universal Mobile Telecommunications System) will give users download speeds of around 380 kbps.

If all this makes you tremble with excitement, then just hold on to your hat a moment. The industry has come up with all sorts of predictions of how, for instance, 270m Europeans will have access to mobile wireless technology by 2005 and that by then 69% of mobile phone users will be using WAP-enabled services to access the Internet. Well, maybe they will, maybe they won't. At the present time there is a distinct lack of suitable services for mobile phones, which is likely to delay the uptake of such technology. Predictions of wide-spread mobile shopping by the middle of 2001 are likely to be vastly over-inflated. But then, again, who knows?

File sharing

What is more likely are some of the predictions for the way in which the Internet itself will change. A new type of technology called peer-to-peer computing looks likely to make a huge impact both in the publishing of on-line information and by extension how this will affect knowledge sharing within a company.

Most of the data accessible over the World Wide Web is held on servers. When you go on-line and browse a Web site, your local computer is effectively accessing that Web server.

With peer-to-peer networking, every computer connected to the Internet has the capacity to act as a server. So any computer which is connected to a centralised network in a company, for instance, can be accessed by any other computer within that company network.

The technology for doing this was developed by American students for disseminating music files across campus networks. Soon a Web site called Napster was set up offering worldwide sharing of audio files using the MP3 format. Although at the time of writing it appears that the all-powerful music industry is set to close Napster down, the cataloguing of each file and the way in which it can be shared across the entire pool of those signed up to Napster's services has demonstrated the potential for the future.

Some Web watchers have suggested that file sharing could turn the entire Internet inside out. Publishing files to the Internet has traditionally required a level of technical ability. But, using this technology, publishing a file could hardly be simpler. Further, as one file is copied by ten people, another ten people can each make a copy of the ten original copies and so on and so on. The effect is a viral-like spread of the original file allowing copying at a phenomenal rate.

It is believed that both AOL and Yahoo! are developing file sharing software to offer their members which, if true, will bring file sharing to the masses. Imagine in a business environment how useful it could be to share, say, architectural drawings or engineering specifications.

File-sharing applications designed with business in mind have already begun to appear. In an office environment, for instance, file sharing can be used to extract and share specific data on one employee's machine with everyone else on the network. Each individual machine periodically interrogates the server for updates. Only this information is shared – as opposed to being able to share anything that resides on every computer's hard disk – and this, combined with the way in which all data is indexed and shared, is what differentiates this type of sharing from just giving everyone access to everyone else's hard disk.

Of course, there will be other major changes in the way the Internet operates within the e-commerce arena in the coming months and years. When you look at how the whole of the Internet has changed out of all recognition in the past five years, it is next to impossible to predict very far ahead as to how we will all be transacting our businesses in the coming decade. What is undeniable, however, is that e-commerce is set to 'invade' every arena of business and no one will be immune to its effects.

CRM and CMR

12

Demanding customers

Flexible companies

Mobile customers

Products and services that customers really want

Customer Relationship Management (CRM) has long been a mantra chanted within business life. However, managing customer relations is not an easy task, however small or large the company, or however wide or narrow the range of products or services offered.

The Internet offers different opportunities and threats to your business's ability to manage its relationships with your customers.

The speed of the Internet and its ordering processes – which enable many more spontaneous purchases as well as just-in-time (or time-critical) purchases – has changed the expectation of the customer as far as speed of delivery is concerned. It is likely therefore that the first complaint to land noisily in someone's ear on the customer relations desk will be that of a customer who thinks you should have delivered what he or she ordered sooner than *you* thought you should.

Demanding customers

In truth, the Internet changes the norms of the past and therefore if a customer is ordering on-line from your e-commerce site and it is an easy and quick process to undertake, he or she will expect that it is an easy and quick process for you to deliver the things ordered. In the days when you had to phone an order through, then send a cheque (which had to be cleared) and then wait for the other paperwork to be completed internally at the supplying company's offices, a wait for dispatch of 28 days was pretty good going. Now, you have to have all your internal processes Web-enabled if you are going to be able to keep your customer wanting what was ordered a mere day or two ago!

This, like all the other processes which can be automated – and therefore Internetted – creates a problem for customer relationships altogether. During the time that the business is moving into using intranets and extranets and going for a full-blown e-commerce solution, the people who will suffer are likely to be the customers – and, as usual, the computers will be given the blame by the customer relations department.

If you focus on the need for good customer relationships whilst you are planning your e-commerce implementation, then the need to tell your customers what is happening and gain their cooperation will be evident. Their cooperation and feedback can then become part of the successful process of transition – and you may get more help than you bargained for, as well as some insight as to what your customers really want from your business.

As we've indicated, the speed of the Internet changes pretty well everything and that includes the relationship between a customer and the company. If we follow the impact of customer perception that the company is making it easy and quick to order it follows that it should be easy and quick to deliver products; the next step is to accept the fact that the customer does not have to be loyal to you at all because of geography any more. Customer loyalty used to be more or less guaranteed by location, price, choice and relationship. Now it is different. Customers are totally spoilt for choice with the Internet bringing them the opportunity to purchase the product they want from almost anywhere for a price that suits them and if you don't look after them then they'll not bother to type in your URL (Web address) again. They will be less tolerant since the Internet gives them more power to choose what they buy, from whom and where.

Customers need to be massaged, not just managed! And, actually, what we have for some time called CRM (Customer Relationship Management) should be renamed – CMR, that is, Customer Managed Relationships.

Now this is a totally different ball game unless you are producing bespoke products or services of some kind.

Ultimately the power is moving from the company to the customer to a greater degree than ever before and so putting your best people on to the customer service side of the business still won't deliver customer loyalty and enable the relationships to be worthwhile without running your people ragged in the process.

Actually, the only way to really make it work is to ensure that everyone in your company knows how to deal with customers and how to build relationships with them. If you leave it to a department then you'll find that their knowledge of where the business is going is left behind and salesmen will sell things that cannot be delivered – either in time or for the price expected, or even to the quality expected. If your customer relations department is always taking complaints then communication between the customers and the other areas of your business needs to be opened up. It will save time, it will save money and it will also save disaffected customer relations people.

Just as an example within the last week of writing this book, Tesco Direct were having trouble with their databases. As we got on-line to place our weekly order, the supply of goods normally available on-line was reduced to a mere 15% of the usual range (for instance there was no unsalted butter available). The guide price given for the order was obviously calculated wrongly

Figure 12.1 Tesco's direct delivery service can't be beaten.

too; but the e-mail confirmation worked and the credit card payment went through without a hitch.

We always choose not to have substitutions for items which are unavailable. The delivery arrived on time, but with many items missing and with substitutions made. Some of the missing items were high turnover non-perishable goods like washing up liquid. So we put in a quick call to the local store at Huntingdon to find out why some of the order was missing. It appeared that some items had not been selected properly by the person going round the store with the picking list, whilst some were genuinely out of stock.

Tesco took full responsibility for their poor performance without any prompting. They immediately refunded the £5 delivery charge and after another hour phoned to say that they had received new stock of some of the missing items. Even though it was 8 o'clock in the evening they made arrangements to bring these around straight away (a distance of 15 miles) and did not charge for them. How we now love Tesco! What can be better than eating free raspberries on an autumn morning – and the fact that our original order was mishandled has been put far behind us. We can only think well of Tesco. Is this an example of brilliant customer relations – or what?

Flexible companies

For a company to survive in the future, let alone make a profit, it needs to have a more flexible approach both to what it sells – whether it be products or services – and to listen to what the customers want. Many a product sale has been made harder because the delivery firm used has been inflexible and totally focused on what it wants, rather than the wants and needs of the customers. Many is the time that people have been expected to take a whole day off just in order to be in to receive a package that could not be given a timed delivery. The delivery company, of course, wants to work out the most economically viable route for the driver but that, even though it affects pricing, should be able to be transmitted to the waiting customer so that a delivery within an hour or two timeframe could be guaranteed. What does this sort of example result in? A customer who was a joyous purchaser becoming unhappy about his purchase simply because the delivery firm would not agree a timetable. Many customers would have preferred a timed delivery option even at a higher cost. Customer satisfaction needs to become paramount if they are going to be loyal.

The delivery company should have the two options available at different costs and the supplier should source contracts with different delivery companies in order to provide maximum customer service to suit the customer.

Perhaps at this juncture you should take a look at your products and services and see what flexibility you could offer your customers?

How you look after your customers can also be helped by the Internet. Apart from being able to get a wealth of information available to them on the Web which they can access and appraise in their own time, transparency of order tracking can save a myriad of chasing phone calls. That alone saves time and money for the company as well as frustration and lack of knowledge for the customer. It puts the whole relationship on a different footing. It is almost like treating a customer as if they were an adult! It sounds strange but many business-to-customer relationships follow the patronising and almost parental model that is perhaps best personified in the relationships between many service garages and female customers.

Mobile customers

The path that the Internet is taking the way we work is more toward mobility. People work in their cars, which are often, in effect, mobile offices. We work with mobile devices and laptop computers which communicate using infrared and will soon have Bluetooth to enable cable-free communications. When the geodesic satellites are in position in 2003 then it will be possible to pinpoint anyone with a mobile communications device to within one square metre across the globe. The opportunities to be there for your customer and for your customer to benefit from you will be very different. So will the opportunities to annoy!

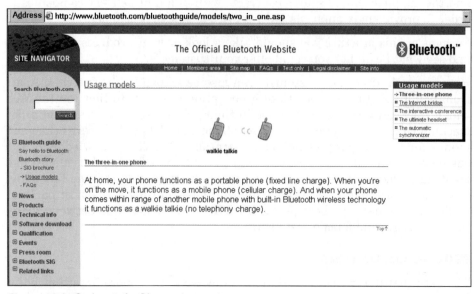

Figure 12.2 Can't wait for Bluetooth to arrive.

But if where we are going is towards mobile customers, be it business or consumer, then we have to be prepared to look after those customers and their needs whilst mobile and not assume that they will go back to the office to receive sheaves of paperwork or log on to a Web site. So our approach to all our communications and sales lines needs to be both cryptic and in-depth to cater for the different communications platforms as well as how much time customers have available.

Products and services that customers really want

The mobile customer will be almost armour-plated. In the same way that you can now switch your mobile phone off and can filter out the advertisements on television channels, customers of the future will be able to filter out the advertisements they don't want to know about. They'll be in a position to say 'No' to your phone calls and other unsolicited calls without getting involved at all.

This turns turtle the whole CRM philosophy because it turns it into CMR and the customer will manage relations only with the companies with whom he or she wants to have a relationship.

How companies develop when armed with this knowledge is up to them. The opportunities are there and the ultimate goal should therefore be to provide products and services that customers actually want – rather than developing products and services which 'should be able to be sold'. How that affects your company is up to you – but e-commerce is the best enabler you can get to put you ahead of the game and provide your customers with what they want.

Index

A

Actinic, 35–6
Add Me, 57
ADSL (asynchronous/asymmetric
    digital subscriber line)
    technology, 64, 78, 116–18
advertising, 54, 60–4
    of contracts and alliances, 103
advertising agencies, 62
advertising standards, 104–5
alliances, 66–7, 103
AlphaCart, 35
AltaVista, 58, 69
Amazon, 10, 67, 72
American Express, 74
Andersen Consulting, 79
anonymity on the Web, 79
AOL, 70, 123
'applications gateways', 78
Ariba.com, 88
auctions on-line, 83–90, 92
    setting-up of, 88
Authority (bureau), 47

B

Bank of America, 74
banner advertisements and banner
    exchange schemes, 61–4, 67, 90
Barclays Merchant Services, 40–1
BCVA, 20
Beenz, 49–50
bidding at auctions, promotion of, 87–8
bidding for contracts, 85
Bidland.com, 88
Big Step, 32
Blair, Tony, 94
Bluetooth, 132
BMW (company), 51
Boeing (company), 93
brand awareness, 61
British Telecom (BT), 49, 117–18
bureau services for credit card
    payments, 43–6
Bureau Veritas, 97
business-to-business transactions,
    9–10, 85

business-to-consumer transactions,
    9–10, 131
    advantages of, 13

C

cable television, 117–18
call centres, 110
car sales, 8
CD Now, 55
'circuit level' system, 78
Clara.net, 27
ClickMiles, 49
commission payments between
    Web sites, 67
compact discs (CDs), 10
competitions, 105
competitors, research on, 19
computer companies, 10
confidential information on the
    Internet, 72, 81
contention ratio, 117
copyright, 105
corporation tax, 101–2
courier companies, 113

credit, 105
credit card issuers, 45
credit card payments, 31, 40–3, 47,
    72–3
  on-line and off-line systems for, 43
currencies, acceptance of, 45
customer relationship management
    (CRM), 126–8, 133
customer-managed relationships
    (CMR), 128, 133
customer service, 8, 36–7
customisation of web sites, 90
CyberCash, 47–8

D

Danzas, 97
data protection, 100
databases
  access to, 18
  connected to web sites, 26, 34
  for marketing, 6
  registration of, 101
Deep Crack, 74
delivery times, 6, 37, 126–7, 130–1
Dell (company), 10–11
Deloitte Touche Tohmatsu, 97
desktop software, 34
disclaimers, 102
distribution channels, 6
domain names, 21–4

expired, 25–6
Double Click, 62
Dun & Bradstreet, 97
dynamic pricing, 84

E

EasyJet, 60
eBay, 85–7
eBits, 49
eCash Technologies, 49
ecBuilder Pro, 35
EDI (electronic data interchange), 6, 93
electronic cash (e-cash), 47–51, 74–5
electronic mail
  content guidelines for, 78
  corporate, 78–81
  monitoring of, 81
  signatures on, 64
eMarketeer, 36
empowerment of customers, 7–8
encryption, 42, 72, 74–6
Euro zone, 51
European e-commerce directive, 108
Excite, 58, 69
expenditure on e-commerce, forecasts
    of, 54, 84–5
extranets, 94, 112–14

F

feedback on clients, 90
file sharing, 123

Finland, 51
firewall protection, 42, 72, 77, 113
  for personal computers, 78
Fireworks software, 36
First Tuesday, 19
First Virtual, 75
flexibility offered to customers, 130–1
Flooz, 49
Ford Motors, 93
Forrester Research, 54
fraud, 42, 72
free gifts, 105
Freeserve, 61, 70

G

gambling, 42, 105
General Electric, 96
Germany, 108
global access to the Internet, 119
global trading, 9
Google, 55–6, 58
government procurement, 94
GPRS (general packet radio
    service), 121
GSM (global standard for mobile
    communications), 121

H

hackers, 42, 74–6
Hewlett-Packard, 93
high-value goods, 42

HomePage Creator, 32
hosting of web sites, 22–8
Hot Bot, 58
hyperlinks, 67, 94

I

Industry To Industry (ITOI), 97
intellectual property rights, 103–4
Internet service providers (ISPs),
     25, 61, 70
intranets, 17, 94, 97, 110–14
investors in new businesses, 19–21
Ipoints, 49
Ireland, 102

J

just in time delivery, 6, 126

K

keywords, 56

L

Labour Party, 77
Land's End, 107–8
LastMinute.com, 49, 67
leased lines, 118
legal jurisdiction in other countries,
     107–8
Letsbuyit.com, 95
libel, 79, 105
licensing, 104–5
LineOne, 70

low-value goods, 47
loyalty schemes, 49
Luxembourg, 101
Lycos, 58, 69

M

marketing 4, 6–7, 18, 54, 102
  joint campaigns, 66
  traditional forms of, 67
'marriage brokers', 6
MasterCard, 74
media companies, 62
merchant services for handling credit
     card payments, 40–3
meta tags, 58
micropayments, 47–51, 74–5
Microsoft, 50
mobile phones, 121–2
Mondex, 47, 49, 74
motivation for buying decisions, 36–7
MP3 format, 105, 122
MSN, 61, 70
music, licensing of, 105

N

Napster, 105–6, 122
NatWest Bank, 47
National (UK) Health Service, 95
National (US) Consumer League, 72
Netbanx, 46
Netscape, 50, 70

newsgroups, 64–6
Northern Light, 58
Norton's Internet Security, 78
Norwich Union, 79
NTSL, 118
NukeNabber, 78

O

open source model, 4
Oracle, 93

P

packet filters, 78
Paint Shop Pro, 36
partnerships, 19, 104
passwords
     for extranets, 113
     for micropayments, 75
payment terms, 102
peer-to-peer computing, 122
Pepsico, 93
PGP (pretty good privacy), 75–6
photographs, use of, 36
pornography, 21, 42
portals, 61–2, 68–70, 88
procurement, electronic, 92–7
project management, 111
PSPs (payment services
     providers), 44–6
public key cryptography, 75

Q

QXL, 85, 89

R

Ready2Shop, 67–8
Real Media, 62
registration
  of customers with trading sites, 72
  of databases under Data Protection
    Act, 100
  of domain names, 21–4, 26
  of sites with portals, 69
  of sites with search directories, 56–7
revenue sharing agreements, 104
revenue streams, 4–6

S

Sainsbury's, 11
satellite downloads, 119
search directories, 54–5, 69
search engines, 54–8, 69
Secure Trading (bureau), 47
security
  on the Internet, 72–81, 92
  of intranets and extranets, 114
server-based web site services, 32–4
SET (secure electronic
    transactions), 74
SGS, 97
Shop in a Box, 35
shop@ssistant, 35

Shopcreator, 32–3
signature files, 64
simultaneous transactions, 44
Site Reporter, 27
smart cards, 47
software for site design, 34–5
Sotheby's, 85
sourcing of supplies, 92, 96
SSL (secure sockets layer), 42, 74
Stainton, Julian, 79
StoreCentre, 32
streaming video, 64, 116
Submit-It, 57
supermarkets, 11–13
supply chain, 6, 93, 113
Swindon, 48

T

technical expertise, need for, 17–18
technical support, offering of, 45
Teledesic, 119–20
television, 116–21
terms and conditions, 102
Tesco, 11, 128–30
'thinking globally, acting locally', 107–8
Thwaite, 75
trademark protection, 21, 103
trading standards, 105–6
trust, 96, 113
24-7 (media company) 62

U

UMTS (universal mobile
    telecommunications system),
    121
Unix software, 26
UOP (company), 79
URLs added to printed matter, 58–60
users of the Internet, number of, ix
USP (unique selling point), 16

V

value added services, 8–9
value added tax (VAT), 45, 101
Vauxhall (company), 8
Verisign, 75
vetting of suppliers and orders, 95–7
Viagra, 21
video banners, 64
video conferencing and video
    messaging, 17
virtual shopping baskets, 32
viruses, 77–8, 81
Visa, 42, 72, 74
Visa Cash, 49, 74
vision statements, 16

W

Wall Street Journal, 5
WAP (wireless application protocol)
    technology, 121

'web cam' cameras, 112
web sites, 2–4
   design of, 30–7
Web Tool Pro, 32
Western Provident Association, 79
Wetlands website, 21

Windows NT software, 26
WinNUKE, 78
wizards, 32
word-of-mouth promotion, 64–5
working capital, sources of, 20–1
WorldPay, 46

Y
Yahoo!, 33, 50, 55, 58, 61–2, 69, 123
Z
Zoom, 49